Time Away

Time Away

A Guide
for Personal Retreat

Ben C. Johnson
Paul H. Lang

UPPER
ROOM BOOKS®
NASHVILLE

Cover design: Bruce Gore / www.gorestudio.com
Cover image: Getty Images
Interior design: Nancy Terzian / www.buckinghorsedesign.com
First printing: 2010

LIBRARY OF CONGRESS CATALOGING-IN-PUBLICATION DATA
Johnson, Ben Campbell.
  Time away : a guide for personal retreat / Ben C. Johnson ; Paul H. Lang.
     p. cm.
  ISBN 978-0-8358-1011-1
  1. Spiritual retreats—Christianity. I. Lang, Paul H. II. Title.
  BV5068.R4J65 2010
  269'.6—dc22   2010005274

Printed in the United States of America

Dedicated to
William Hulitt Gloer

Contents

Preface

This book will help you make a personal retreat. You will find here good resources for planning and making the most of such a time away. The chapters clarify what a retreat is, how to prepare for it, how to plan your time, and how to reenter your world after the retreat. One chapter offers guidance for a retreat at a monastery or convent, introducing the idea to those who have not made a monastic retreat and exploring monastic life at greater depth for those who have.

My friend Dr. Paul Lang assisted in writing this book. Now a Presbyterian minister in Greenville, North Carolina, Paul was a student of mine in seminary. He provided the chapter on monastic retreats and appendix B, The Offices of Lauds and Compline. He also has made significant contributions to the other chapters. I appreciate his valuable work.

We envision this book first as a step-by-step guide for individuals in deciding to make a retreat, planning it, doing it, and reentering day-to-day life after the retreat. Second, it will introduce monastic life and the daily Hours of Prayer into the lives of retreatants and also into the worship of churches (see appendix B). Third, this book can serve as a text for teaching members of a congregation the value and purpose of personal retreats and how to plan them (see appendix A). Fourth, retreat leaders will find insights and exercises beneficial to participants in a directed retreat (see appendix C). Chapters 1 and 2 feature personal stories of retreats from a variety of people to inspire and motivate.

Just a word about how this book came into being. In the spring of 2007 I had a weeklong retreat at Christ in the Desert in Abiquiu, New Mexico. While I was there, I wanted to see a new guesthouse at the monastery which had been funded by a friend of mine. But it so happened that a professor from Baylor University's George W. Truett Theological Seminary in Waco, Texas, had reserved the room for the week—Dr. William Hulitt Gloer.

I met Dr. Gloer and asked if I might visit him and see the room my friend had underwritten. He graciously consented. When I approached the new addition, he was sitting in the yard looking at the mountains in the distance. We shook hands, and he asked me if I were the same Ben Johnson who taught at Columbia Theological Seminary in Decatur, Georgia. I said that I was. He asked if I would be willing to speak about making a retreat to a dozen students he had brought to the monastery.

I did meet with the students and shared a few insights. As I prepared to leave, Hulitt inquired, "Have you ever written about how to make a personal retreat?" I shook my head. "Well, you ought to," he commented.

After I left, a strange thing happened. I found myself thinking about the question, *If I were to write a book on making a personal retreat, what would I say?* Ideas began coming into my mind, tumbling in one after the other. I pulled out a yellow pad and started writing them down. Before I realized it, this book was birthing itself. When I decided to include a chapter on monastic retreats, Paul Lang came to mind because he has written about the topic with deep understanding. And I believe his explanation of the Liturgy of the Hours as a form of prayer will spread to a number of churches in the next decade.

Beyond what Paul and I have done to write this book, in some sense this book belongs to Dr. William Hulitt Gloer, and for that reason we dedicate it to him.

Ben Campbell Johnson
Professor Emeritus of Christian Spirituality
Columbia Theological Seminary

CHAPTER ONE

What Is a Retreat?

* *

*Retreat is a deliberate attempt to place your life before God
to seek a deeper awareness of the Divine Presence.*

What do you do on a retreat? Some years ago a friend of mine came to town unexpectedly, arriving on a day I had set aside for time away on retreat. I invited him to join me.

"What are we going to do for a full day?" he asked.

"Pray," I responded.

He blurted out, "It doesn't take me that long to pray."

I suggested that the day might be different from what he imagined. Sure enough it was. On the way home, after reflecting on the experience, my friend commented, "That was the shortest day I ever spent!"

Retreat, for some, is a corrupted word. To many persons it is a catchall term that covers gatherings for planning, teaching, choir rehearsals, leadership development, and a variety of efforts to enrich the church. All these are good endeavors and have their place, but they are not retreats in the sense that we are using the word. For others the word has been corrupted by lectures and counseling that created guilt and remorse, followed by the promise of forgiveness and cleansing through prayer and confession.

A retreat is a time to discern the reason for your life. It is not "running away" from hard issues but rather taking time to face those issues. Actually a time in the desert is more an advance than a withdrawal.

Retreat is not a permanent withdrawal from conflicts and the struggles of life; it is not playing the coward with your problems. Retreat is a temporary withdrawal to be renewed, to regroup, and to find the strength that you need to go forward. It is a temporary disengagement from your daily routine to place yourself before God so that you can reengage your life and work with greater insight, energy, and purpose.

DISCOVERING THE VALUE OF TIME AWAY

Perhaps my experience is unique, but maybe not. I had been on my spiritual quest for a couple of decades before ever making a personal retreat. Possibly you too have traveled a good distance on your spiritual journey without making a retreat. I was at least halfway through my pilgrimage on earth before I learned anything about a regular time to be away from the routine of life in order to focus my attention upon God and God's intention for me. But over the past forty years I have found the practice of regularly planning time away of great value, and thus I want to share with you what this sort of experience is and what it can do for you. Three retreat experiences have been crucial to my growth and to my following the path that God has willed for me.

CALL FOR A DECISION

The first of these retreats took place in 1963 when I was pastor of a church in a small Alabama town, Phenix City. God had used me to initiate a rather dynamic weekend event, the Lay Witness Mission, and I had visions of following through with its development. The drive within was so strong that I felt I was being called to this work.

The call seemed to point toward further training, and in obedience I began seeking admission to the PhD program at Emory University in Atlanta, Georgia. If I got accepted in the program, I had enough money to pay the first year's tuition, but I didn't have funds for a house, for food, and for taking care of my family's needs. As the sense of call deepened and the anxiety about how I could respond to it expanded, I felt an immense need for God's assurance. I was driven to prayer.

When the tension grew to the breaking point, I decided to pray all night in the sanctuary of the church I was serving. Why couldn't I pray at home? Why couldn't I pray during the day? I could have done both, but something in my background caused me to feel that praying all night offered God a more earnest approach on my part than praying at my own convenience. So I set aside a night to pray from dark to dawn; I took only the Bible into that retreat in the church's sanctuary; and hour after hour I prayed and waited for some word, some sense of assurance, and clarity of direction from the Lord.

I began reading in Genesis, and I came to the story of Abram. After his father died, he received direction from God.

> Now the LORD said to Abram, "Go from your country and your kindred and your father's house to the land that I will show you. I will make of you a great nation, and I will bless you, and make your name great, so that you will be a

A Huge Exhale

For me a retreat is like being a frantic world traveler who wants nothing more in life than to return to my humble home, curl up in God's lap, rest my head on his shoulder and eat oatmeal. Retreat gives me permission to be a centered self in a world where I am primarily someone's mother, wife, daughter, sister, boss, employee or friend. . . . Retreat is permission from God and my busy world to be selfish for a bit. It is like one huge exhale!

—a contemplative

blessing. I will bless those who bless you, and the one who curses you I will curse; and in you all the families of the earth shall be blessed."

So Abram went, as the Lord had told him; and Lot went with him.—Genesis 12:1-4

These words gripped my mind. As I pondered them, it seemed God was calling me to leave the place where I had ministered for five years and to go to the place that God would show me. Just as God had blessed Abram, I could expect God to bless me.

This text reminded me of another person's reflection on Abram's obedience. In the letter to the Hebrews the author wrote: "By faith Abraham obeyed when he was called to set out for a place that he was to receive as an inheritance; and he set out, not knowing where he was going" (Heb. 11:8). This text showed me that Abram believed God was calling him, and he trusted God's promise enough to leave the security of his place. The words that seemed to enlighten and liberate me were "not knowing." Abraham set out "not knowing" where he was going. I knelt at the Communion rail where I had prayed many times before. As God's promise soaked into my soul, I gained the confidence to "set out, not knowing" but trusting that God was calling and that all my needs would be supplied.

I had just experienced a six- or seven-hour

> ### *Time to Be with God*
>
> *When I have spent time in retreat, I usually take away from the experience these things: a clearer focus, greater insight into God and myself, increased energy, renewed soul, a greater awareness of the presence of God, a reminder of the awesome providence of God, release from heavy burdens, an awareness that I am a beloved child of God, and strength for the journey.*
>
> —a pastor

retreat before I knew how to define the word. It came out of my decision to get away and to devote my time wholly to God when I did not know anything about structuring time or various ways to pray. The decision to move to Atlanta and to enter the PhD program at Emory University proved to be one that would change my life forever. I believe it was those hours of prayer in the church that night that empowered me to make this risky decision and to follow through with the consequences that flowed from it.

CALL OF THE DESERT

I first began to think about going to the desert when I read a book by Carlo Carretto. I had never heard of the man before the day I thumbed through a catalog and saw the title of his book *Letters from the Desert*. The title fascinated me enough to order it. I recall the Saturday morning when I opened this book and read the first few pages. In that moment I knew that between the covers of that paperback God was waiting to speak to me. I read Carlo's stories with the hunger of a man who had been on a fast for forty days.

It was Brother Carlo who inspired me to go to the desert where I could find a place of quiet and solitude and listen to God and to my own soul. I gave much thought to this journey to the desert and inquired of others where a desert retreat might be made. A spiritual friend and guide mentioned a monastery in New Mexico, Christ in the Desert, and I made plans to go there.

On Memorial Day weekend in 1986 my wife and I were relaxing in a condo on the Gulf of Mexico. She was sitting on the balcony watching the waves roll in and having her first cup of coffee. Without premeditation I stepped out on the deck and heard these words coming out of my mouth: "Next June I am going to the desert for a month." Before I realized what I had said, she responded, "Why don't you just stay the whole summer?" If I had thought only once, I never would have made a statement like that before Nan had had her second cup of coffee. After we talked about it, she was fine with my doing the retreat, but I botched it with my abrupt announcement.

During the next twelve months a strange thing happened. Every day at an odd moment without my intending it, I thought about going to the desert, making the retreat at Christ in the Desert Monastery. The notion that this was an important event in my life deepened as the weeks went by. Often I wondered what I would be doing during this period of time. Why was I going on this retreat? By the first of the year, it had come to me that during my weeks away, I was to pray about the rest of my life. To strengthen my resolve and to absorb my purpose more completely, I decided to leave off wine or any alcohol for the year. At parties and social events of all kinds, I kept the resolution and on each occasion recalled my commitment to spend an extended time with God.

On this second retreat in 1987, I spent two weeks at Christ in the Desert, the Benedictine monastery just north of Abiquiu, New Mexico. By then I had been reading other writings by Carlo Carretto in addition to *Letters from the Desert.* The desert offered many gifts to Brother Carlo; going to the desert and joining the Little Brothers of Jesus, an order founded by Charles de Foucauld, was like a ten-year retreat for him. His account of this experience made me want to find my own desert and spend my time with God. Here is a sampling of passages from Brother Carlo's writings that resonated with me during this period:[1]

> When I was forty-four years old, there occurred the most serious call of my life: the call to the contemplative life. . . . This time I had to say "yes" without understanding a thing. "Leave every-thing and come with me into the desert. It is not your acts and deeds that I want; I want your prayer, your love."

> The great joy of the Saharan novitiate is the solitude, and the joy of solitude—silence, true silence, which penetrates everywhere and invades one's whole being, speaking to the soul with wonderful new strength unknown to men to whom this silence means nothing.

I have come into the desert to pray, to learn to pray. It has been the Sahara's great gift to me, and I should like to share it with all my friends. It is immeasurable and contains every other gift within itself. It is the *sine qua non* of life, the treasure buried in the field, the pearl of great price discovered in the market.

Much that I feared about this time of silence and the extended time away from Nan and home did not happen. The silence did not frighten me; I did not get into depths of my soul that I could not handle; I did not become bored; I felt purpose and meaning in each day, and my life became a prayer.

At the time I was fifty-five years old; and as I began to pray about the remainder of my life, it seemed to unfold in my mind. I was guided to begin teaching Christian spirituality at Columbia Theological Seminary, leaving behind my position there as the professor of evangelism and church growth.

On Pentecost Sunday of 1987 I was praying about the end of my life. I envisioned the year, the gathering of children, and saying goodbye. I felt no fear. My expectations about the future beyond this life rose higher. I committed my whole life to God.

As I look back over the past twenty years, the vision that came to me in the desert has beautifully materialized. I did become professor of Christian spirituality at Columbia Theological Seminary, and the work in Christian spirituality was a crowning gift to my twenty years of teaching. Direction and meaning in my life were the gifts of the desert.

CALL TO A NEW WORK

The third notable retreat occurred in May of 1995. I had just been appointed professor of Christian spirituality for the next academic year. The weeklong retreat provided a transition from teaching evangelism and church growth to teaching Christian spirituality. I did not know how to pray about the new opportunity. I wanted God's blessing, but I did not want my time at the Monastery of the Holy Spirit in Conyers, Georgia, to be self-serving. I asked Father Anthony, "Do you think it is right for me to pray for the success of the spirituality emphasis at the seminary?" He was quick to answer, "If you are doing it for the glory of God, it is."

That week was the first time I chanted the Psalms with the monks. Father Anthony asked me if I would like to sit by him and join the monks in the Daily Office. When I responded enthusiastically, he showed me the right book and the right place—and also told me not to sing too loudly. During the week my vision for the next year shifted; I was drawn more deeply into the life of the monks; I felt a renewing of my spirit; and I resolved to come to the monastery each month to rediscover who I was and what my life was about.

My purpose in describing these retreats is to illustrate three experiences of time away in retreat. In each instance the issue for me was vocation, my calling. In Phenix City, Alabama, I simply followed my heart and what I believed a serious man in my circumstance would do. I prayed about how best to serve God with my whole life. When I went away to the desert at age fifty-five, again I was praying for clarity in my vocation for the remainder of my career. I felt led by God to be away for an extended period of time. In the third retreat, a week in length, prior to becoming professor of Christian spirituality, I sought clarity, empowerment, and direction in initiating this new emphasis at the seminary.

These retreats centered on searching for God's will or the meaning of my life or direction on new stages in the journey. I have emphasized the vocational aspect of the time away because each of these deserts came at a significant crossroad in my life. But surely these times were as much about meaning, direction, and God's will as they were about vocation. I underscore these various aspects, which were simultaneously present in the retreats, to make it clear that a trip to the desert is never about just one thing—meaning, direction in life, God's will, fulfillment, renewal, and refreshment are likely all present.

A DEEPER LOOK AT RETREATS

A retreat is a specific period of time set aside for God; it may include reading books, resting, reading the Bible, prayer, worship, exercise, and meeting with a spiritual guide. But at the core of a retreat lies the decision to place yourself before God for an uninterrupted period of time.

THE LENGTH OF A RETREAT

A retreat may be of various lengths, from a few hours to a week or, in special circumstances, a month or more. It is up to you to choose the length of time that works best for you. Generally, it is wise to begin with a briefer time and learn ways to work with your life situation and listen to God than to begin with too much time away. Since it is a time of being with God, there are always wonderful surprises. Remember! The quality of the experience rather than the length of time is most important.

A retreat of a few hours might include spending a night away from home alone. This is preferable to a daylong retreat because it gives you a bit more time to step out of your ordinary day into a sacred space you have created. The night becomes an ally and works for your benefit. Powerful insights often arise while we sleep. In an overnight, get to your place, get settled in, and focus on your time away. Keep in mind that a retreat puts you in a new venue so that you may see with new vision.

A longer retreat of five to seven days offers even greater opportunity for silence and reflection on issues of concern. So much more can happen in the weeklong experience; you have time to get settled, develop a routine, and to engage your life in depth. When you are engaged in serious work, the time goes swiftly. In a longer retreat you will find yourself getting more genuinely involved with your life and gaining more insights into your self and your situation.

To spend a month on retreat sounds impossible to many of us who are rushed and busy. It would simply be too much "desert" for us. The longer retreat is not the place to begin. Let your first time away be of a length you can handle and, perhaps, on another occasion expand the duration of retreat.

RETREATS ARE ABOUT MEETING GOD

In retreats humans aim to meet the Holy; the human spirit engages the Holy Spirit—the holy and the human touch each other. Usually this encounter is mediated through the Bible or beauty or memory or a spontaneous thought; this simple awakening to reality may occur through another person, silence, an image or vision, or listening to the voice of God speaking in the soul.

Retreat is not a permanent withdrawal from the conflicts and struggles of life, not playing the coward with one's problems.

Henri Nouwen spoke of the contemporary misunderstanding of solitude as a "private therapeutic place," a "spiritual property for which we can compete on the free market of spiritual goods." We think of solitude as a place where we gather strength to compete in the struggles of life. The retreat is the decision to meet God and to permit the transformation that the Spirit alone can effect; it is not a place to strengthen ourselves to compete with others.[2]

> ### *An Observation Point*
>
> *The military image of a pullback from a forward position in battle has always seemed apt for me. . . . We pull back in order to better reengage in the battle and struggle of life. Among all the gifts of a retreat, I especially appreciate solitude. . . . During a retreat I receive rest from the noise pollution that constantly bombards my ear with words and music, to say nothing of the horns, whistles, and loud motors.*
>
> *—a ranger*

AN IMPORTANT KEY: SILENCE

To be with God, we must learn the power of silence to communicate God's presence. John of the Cross once said, "Silence is God's first language." God speaks the language of silence. If we are to hear the silent voice of God, we must learn to turn down the noise in our lives. The silence of the place does us little good unless we are able to match it with the silence of our souls. The following story about one of the desert fathers, Abbot Macarius, speaks to this point.

Once when Abbot Macarius had given a blessing to the brethren in the church at Scete, he said to them, "Brothers, flee." One of the old men answered him, "How can we flee further than this,

> *Favorite Places for Solitude*
>
> *I need to be alone. I can hear from God when I am alone and processing that time through scripture and journaling. My favorite places to seek solitude are backpacking in the woods and at monasteries. . . . I try to make a two-day retreat once a quarter to process my life.*
>
> —a young disciple

seeing that we are already here in the desert?" Then Macarius placed his finger on his mouth and said, "Flee from this." And with that he entered his cell and shut the door.[3]

CHAPTER TWO

Why Go on a Retreat?

....

God is part of you and your life, and a retreat
will help you notice and acknowledge the presence of God.

One morning I had breakfast with a surgeon who was under considerable stress. After listening to him for about an hour, I commented, "I think you need a retreat at the monastery or some quiet place to help you get your life in order." He responded that he had so much work that such a retreat would be impossible; his partners would never agree to his taking time to go sit in the woods.

"What do you think would happen," I asked, "if suddenly you had paralysis in your right hand and you were unable to operate?" Becoming a bit more specific, I asked, "Do you think the world would stop? Would there be anyone who would handle your tasks?" He must have gotten the point because in a few weeks he went away to ponder his life. While he was away in the fresh air of north Georgia, he made several life-altering decisions.

A retreat will enable you to address the "big questions" in your life. Some of those questions might be: Does my life matter? What am I here for? Does God care about me and my issues? Am I making the right decisions? What do I really value? Is God real? Can I make conscious contact with God? Does God want to be intimately involved in my life? Can God help me with my decisions?

You may admit that time to ponder the major questions of life would be beneficial, but you argue, "I can't do it; I'm too busy, I have too many commitments, I have more pressure than anyone can imagine." Is it possible that some of us are afraid to stop our overly burdened lives and listen to our hearts? Anthony de Mello, a Jesuit priest from India, writes, "Someone once said, 'I dare not stop to think, because if I did, I wouldn't know how to get started again.'"[1]

Having time to deal with yourself is more important than most any other activity you could be engaged in. Yes, more important than work. More important than family. More important than finishing up a list of tasks that should have been done yesterday. All these plans, relationships, and responsibilities are certainly significant and demanding, but each can be handled so much better and more easily if your life is focused.

What reason could compel a person to cease all "productive" activity, step out of the existing web of relationships like family, work, and social connections to go away for a day, a few days, or a week? Let me offer seven reasons why time away from the routine is a good idea:

1. A personal retreat will help you attain balance in your life. Life gets out of equilibrium so easily. For high achievers who are focused on goals, driven by work or the lust for success, keeping life balanced requires a great deal of discipline. All else gets sacrificed to achieve academic, economic, financial, or political aims. High rollers often allow achievement of these goals to spin of control. Personal needs for rest and relaxation are sacrificed in the process, and family also gets lost in the surge to achieve. How could three or four days in a cabin in the woods help a person who is driven in this way? Such a choice in a busy, overcrowded world seems to be a waste of time and a diversion from life's most sought-after destinations or objectives.

Wait! Are these success-driven goals, and the engagement that they require, contributing to a wholesome fulfilled life? Is success worth the price being paid? If these questions catch your attention, a time away could be quite valuable. A time set aside will give you space to look at your life: who you are and what you are doing. Some of the suggestions and exercises that I recommend will draw you into this arena.

On the other hand, some people are adrift, not driven but drifting. For those who lack focus and purpose, a retreat offers an opportunity to listen to their souls. Deep inside, a voice waits to speak; and the word it speaks will bring a sense of purpose and direction. The same exercises that calm the compulsive will energize and direct the aimless.

2. A retreat offers time and space to deal with the persistent questions of your life. When did you last ask yourself, *What is the meaning of my life?* And when did you ponder that question until you stretched it the length of your earthly sojourn?

Many of us run so fast that a question like this seldom has a chance to occupy space in our consciousness. Suppressing this soul-searching question drives our life's pace faster and faster, and reflection on the meaning of our life gets squeezed out by demands, schedules, and other packed agendas. At the other extreme, some of us circle the question endlessly without ever discerning a way forward.

What would happen if for one whole day you lived with the *why* question about each aspect of your life? Proceed to ask why to every answer that you give yourself. If you persist in asking the why question, you will begin to break open your life; and if you are honest with yourself, you will discover the values that drive your life! A time of reflection offers you a path to freedom from unconscious forces that control your life. If you don't set aside time to think about these big questions, you'll likely miss out on some very consequential aspects of what your life is meant to be.

3. A personal retreat offers an opportunity to look at relationship issues in your life. Life is made up of relationships—family, friends, and colleagues. Conflicts and wasted energy usually stem from relationships with the people in your life. By living fast-paced lives or mired, out-of-focus lives, you may avoid facing marred or broken relationships until they reach a crisis point. Are your significant relationships worth taking time to sort out, to value, and to smooth their rough edges?

4. Time away will lead you to the rhythm of your life. A joyous and fulfilled life relies on finding your personal rhythm —the ebb and flow. Life, like a river, ebbs and flows with breakneck rapids and still pools. A thousand distractions and challenges get us out of the flow of our lives—stress, high demands, marching to another person's drumbeat rather than your own. Intelligent, successful, hardworking people get out of sync with themselves—their body, their psyche, and their spiritual rhythm. When we are out of sync, everything we do takes more effort and greater energy.

A retreat time allows you to recover your rhythm and get into the flow of your life. It encourages this alignment in several ways—coping with your issues, facing your questions, and helping you find the center. Your personal center is that arena where you find rest, consciously meet your destiny, and achieve balance. A retreat operates like a clock with two power sources. On a retreat you "pull the plug," and the batteries keep the time going while you are checking and resetting your internal gauges. The result is equivalent to being reborn—a second, third, or fourth chance with your life's direction. Resetting your life is not too difficult. If you slow down enough, things may automatically readjust. The silence and stillness of a retreat, like magnets, will draw you into the flow of meaning, improve your reading of internal yearnings; and when you begin to go with the energy within, you can draw the activities of your life into the rhythm you have established. So if you desire to open to the currents of energy in your life, find a place of retreat to get into the groove.

5. Withdrawal from the routine of normal daily life gives you an opportunity to clarify your perspective, perhaps even acquire a totally new perspective. Does your perception of your situation or goals often become blurred? Do you focus too close in or too far from matters of consequence? Do the lenses through which you view life make it seem too difficult or even impossible to find true happiness and fulfillment? Take your present circumstances, for example. Perhaps you can see no way to correct a relationship or deal with an impossible task or make a major decision. You may drive through the day in confusion, or you have a conflict with your partner, or you have ungrateful children, or your work has become boring, or retirement has become meaningless: there seems to be no way out of your predicament.

Amazing things can occur on a retreat that allow you see through new eyes. It is surprising how much energy wells up when you slow down, discover the center of your being, and begin to reclaim the power that you have projected on the obstacles that stand in your way. As you honestly face the conflicts in your life and make new decisions, situations begin to change. Remember: life is what it is and no amount of dreaming and wishing will change it, but new decisions will!

A friend found himself bound by his circumstances. He had lived twenty years with an emotionally ill wife; his kids didn't understand his choices; he felt blocked in making decisions that would free him from old commitments, and he was depressed. In a time away from his daily routine, he began to see himself and his circumstances in a new light; he discovered that he was free to make new choices about family, business, and his future. I doubt that this release from the bondage of his accustomed life would have happened if he had not availed himself of time away in a different space.

6. The rhythm of engagement and withdrawal is built into the nature of reality. The sun rises, giving light in the morning, and then retreats into darkness in the evening; bears search for food and eat voraciously in spring and summer and then hibernate in winter; humans are to labor six days and withdraw from work on the seventh for rest. When we ignore this aspect of balance, soon we are consumed with issues, unresolved questions, and the anxiety that emerges from inner conflict.

Perhaps you need to consider a retreat because you were made for both engagement and withdrawal—engagement with the world and life and withdrawal to be renewed and re-created. In the Creation story, this profound truth is modeled in the action of God who labored for six days and rested on the seventh. What kind of Superman or Wonder Woman would it take to say, "God may need withdrawal and rest, but I don't!"

7. Time away allows you to establish, reestablish, or expand your consciousness of God in yourself and in the universe. This truth lies at the center of the need for retreat. God is the source of meaning, power, and value in the world and in our lives. The monotheistic religions Christianity, Judaism, and Islam all attest to the fact that

> ## To Know Myself
>
> *When I take a personal retreat, I am setting aside a period of time to build my relationship with God. This relationship has two aspects: growth in self-knowledge and growth in the knowledge of God. . . . Knowledge of self and the knowledge of God exist in a mutually supportive way. I once heard someone say that when Walter Hilton, an Englishman and spiritual writer, says that when we come to know ourselves as we really are, it will not be long before we come to know God as God really is.*
>
> —a writer

God is the center of life and meaning. God spoke through Muhammad: "Praise be to God, Lord of the Universe, the Compassionate, the Merciful, Sovereign of the Day of Judgment! You alone we worship, and to You alone we turn for help" (Koran 1:2-5). So Islam says, "You alone we worship, and to You alone we turn for help."

The Hebrew scripture says: "Hear, O Israel: The LORD is our God, the LORD alone. You shall love the LORD your God with all your heart, and with all your soul, and with all your might. Keep these words that I am commanding you today in your heart" (Deut. 6:4-6).

> ## For an Extended Sabbath
>
> *For me, a retreat is a time set apart to be reminded of God's presence in a deeper way. It is a time to remember again that God holds the world and me. It is a time to relax into God's sovereignty and to remember God's activity, not my own. It is a time that restores the rhythm for me between work and rest. As I think on it, for me retreat is extended Sabbath.*
>
> —a mother, wife

In conversation with an inquiring mind, Jesus restated the same standard. So Christianity says, "'You shall love the LORD your God with all your heart, and with all your soul, and with all your mind.' This is the greatest and first commandment. And a second is like it: 'You shall love your neighbor as yourself'" (Matt. 22:37-39).

These statements represent the core of religion for half the earth's population. The love of God attracts us, purifies us, and clarifies our vision of ourselves and of the world. Occasionally we need to stop and rediscover our relationship with the source of our being.

I have no interest in seeking to prove to you the existence and nature of God, but I do have a passion for helping you experience God more fully. I know God has encountered you many times, in many ways and places; and though you did not always recognize the Divine Presence, God has certainly been present in your life. Every breath, every step, and every relationship is imbued with the Spirit of God whether you recognize it or not. Your connection with God goes two ways: you reach out to God, only to discover that God has been reaching out to you for a much longer time.

I have shared the strongest reasons I know for making a retreat. The retreat offers a place to find balance, to deal with life's big questions, to examine the issues in your life, to find the rhythm of your life, to clarify or change perspectives, to get your life more congruent with the structure of reality, and to expand your consciousness of God—the center of power and meaning in the universe. Do these reasons for a retreat begin to persuade you that a time away—outside the bounds of your ordinary days or weeks—just might be what you most need today?

CHAPTER THREE

Preparing for a Retreat

....

When you begin your preparation, you begin your retreat.

Jumping into a three- or four-day retreat without preparing your mind and heart would be like diving into a mountain lake—the change in temperature would be shocking. This shock therapy might be good for some of us, but there are better ways to begin a retreat. Before you leave for a retreat, think about your time away and get your mind around it. If you have only three days, for example, your time will be much richer and more fruitful if you have taken a week or two in advance to prepare your mind and heart for this special time consecrated to God.

Preparation has three aspects: physical, relational, and spiritual. Physical preparation begins with the outward matters of your readiness—like the state of your health. Persons who are not in excellent health surely can make retreats, but they must consider their limitations and how they are to be handled. The relational dimension focuses on those persons in your life who will be affected by your being away. Finally, the spiritual preparation relates to preparing your heart to receive what God intends for you.

Physical Preparation

Preparing the physical aspect of retreating offers a healthy grounding in the earth and earthiness, and addressing these matters relieves pressures on you later. Use this checklist to attend to these particulars.

1. Choose the place for your retreat. Whether you plan to use a cabin in the mountains, a friend's beach house, a state park, a retreat center, or a campsite, make the necessary arrangements. You may need to get keys and learn about special features of the space so that the transition is smooth. If you will be going to a retreat center or a monastery, make reservations and find out the details of checking in and out of the facility. Know the arrangements for bed linens, towels and washcloths, meals and other refreshments.

2. Determine what clothing you will need. The time of year and the place will dictate the clothes you need to pack. If you are headed for a cabin in the woods, you don't need dressy clothes, but if you will be interacting with other persons, you probably want to take something other than your most faded jeans. Some retreat centers and monasteries have guidelines for appropriate dress. For example, monasteries often request that persons not wear shorts. Be sure to check out the dress requirements if you go to a retreat center.

> ### Catching Up
>
> *Andre Gide, who used to travel through the jungles of Africa, often hired native guides to travel with him. One morning after a particularly long day, he prepared to set out again, but the native guides sat down in a circle and refused to leave the camp. When Gide told them to get moving, they replied, "Don't hurry us. We are waiting for our souls to catch up with us."*
>
> —a physician

Consider the temperature differences at noon and early evening. It will be hard to get relaxed and quiet if your teeth are chattering.

3. *Take into account the distance you will travel.* Avoid putting yourself under pressure. You don't want to begin your retreat like an out-of-breath marathon runner. Allow sufficient time for travel; arrive relaxed, and settle quietly into your place.

4. *Make arrangements for food.* If you select a retreat center, food will be provided, but if you are going camping or to a private home, plan what to take with you. You will discover that food will be less important than usual because other issues will take precedence. Fruit, simple breakfast food, and easy-to-prepare meals will add to the effectiveness of your time away.

5. *Decide how long you will be away.* The number of days you will be on retreat will affect choices about clothing, food, family, and perhaps coworkers. Set aside the length of time that seems right for you.

6. *Choose a quiet location.* A house next to railroad tracks or a campsite next to a playground won't be conducive to retreat. If you cannot hear the silence, you will miss the solitude that you seek.

Checklist for Physical Preparation
   a. Choose the place.
   b. Determine what clothing to take.
   c. Plan your travel time.
   d. Make arrangements for food.
   e. Decide the length of your time away.
   f. Choose a quiet location.

RELATIONAL PREPARATION

Relationships matter, and they matter especially with respect to your retreat. You will take your relationships with you. Physical absence from the most important people in your life does not mean that they have lost their influence on you.

1. Negotiate with your significant other. If you are married or have a significant other in your life, negotiating the time, place, and length of stay will clear the way for a wholesome retreat. By the same token, leaving behind an unhappy partner will likely give a great deal of power to anxious, noisome thoughts. Knowing that someone who loves you holds you before God in prayer, knowing that this person is supporting you in your quest and will be eager to hear about your experiences will both protect and energize you.

Your negotiations may include times to check in. While I emphasize rather strongly the necessity to leave your ordinary life behind and give your full attention to the retreat, there is no reason not to check in to see how things are going at home. When I went to Christ in the Desert twenty years ago, my wife's inability to contact me created a great deal of pressure for her. Forsaking a spouse without a clear understanding is not a good thing. A loving gesture surely cannot destroy the mood and atmosphere of a retreat.

2. Be thoughtful of your children if you have them. Most children and youth will be quite curious why you would go away alone for two or three days. Once when I was planning an extended retreat, I discussed it with our children, who were then in their teens. They asked me numerous questions about where I was going and why I felt the need to go so far away. I felt pleased that they cared enough to raise these questions. Their questions helped me to clarify my aims and motives. When I returned, they all were eager to know what happened while I was away.

3. Your coworkers benefit from information about your plans. This gesture on your part will be especially appreciated if your departure will cause changes in their responsibilities. When discussing your plans, though, do not flaunt your decision to go on retreat or make it a matter of pride. Jesus spoke about our not exercising our devotion to be seen by others, and certainly a retreat is not intended to impress someone else.

4. Other connections. There may well be other people who deserve to know about your absence. For example, if a civic or church committee meeting falls during your retreat, let the chairperson know that you will be absent. Do you have volunteer or church responsibilities that will be affected? Find substitutes as appropriate and inform those who need to know about the change.

5. *Fear of loneliness.* It is important to be comfortable with yourself and the silence and solitude that your time away will afford you. Once when I planned an extended retreat, I wondered what would happen to me during the hours of silence. But rather than threatening, I found the silence deeply healing; the dark side that I feared would erupt remained rather placid. The silence of the retreat is healing and liberating, so let yourself flow with the unfolding pattern.

Checklist for Relational Preparation
   a. Negotiate with your significant other.
   b. Consider children and their needs.
   c. Inform coworkers as necessary.
   d. Care for your other responsibilities.
   e. Examine your fears of loneliness and silence.

Spiritual Preparation

Spiritual preparation is also vital for a meaningful retreat. These general instructions will assist in spiritual readiness for your time away:

1. *State the purpose of your retreat.* If nothing more, ask yourself: *What am I seeking; what do I need in my life to be a more faithful servant of God?* If you get no further than asking the question, it is worth asking. In most instances, however, a need, an issue, or an opportunity will become part of the answer to your question of purpose. For many years I went monthly to the Monastery of the Holy Spirit for renewal because I was weary from travel and empty from speaking and teaching. Then, as I have already related, I came to a period of transition into teaching spirituality in the seminary, and I scheduled a week's retreat to listen to God's direction.

Whether or not you are able to state a clear reason for taking time out, merely seeking the reason will have a beneficial effect.

2. *Read before and during your retreat.* Two good books: the Bible, and *A Guide to Prayer for Ministers and Other Servants* (see bibliography for details and other recommendations.). If it is not already a part of your daily discipline, begin to read the Bible; pray for the purpose of your retreat to be revealed to you. You might note in the first three Gospels the times when Jesus went away to the desert for quiet reflection and how he invited his disciples to rest.

Praying the Psalms will also prepare you for your time away. Every human emotion finds expression in these ancient prayers. Pray the Psalms and very soon you will be praying your life. Take a modern translation of the Bible with you and make it the center of your reading.

A Guide to Prayer for Ministers and Other Servants and two more volumes in the series provide an order for daily worship and reflection; quotations from ancient and modern spiritual writers offer material to prompt your reflections and deepen your meditation. These resources will serve you well whether you are gone for a week or a single day.

3. *Keep a journal.* The practice of writing your thoughts and feelings will enable you to think on paper and keep a permanent record of your reflections. To begin this spiritual discipline you need only a notebook or a bound record book and a pen (not a pencil). Journal writing works best when you adopt a receptive posture that allows ideas to arise in your mind and flow out onto the paper. Don't work hard at the task; let it happen. Before you depart for your retreat, find a quiet place where you will not be disturbed and respond to these three questions:

   a. Why am I going on this retreat? (Be still, listen, and write what comes to you.)
   b. What do I hope to receive from my time with God?
   c. God, what would you say to me as I prepare my mind and heart? (Sit quietly and let the thoughts flow into your mind and write them in your journal. Don't force the words; let them come to you.)

This type of writing prepares you to go on the retreat. You are practicing an exercise you will use during your time away.

4. *Pray about your retreat, your time away.* Two kinds of prayer will provide good preparation. First, ask God for what you most deeply desire from this time set aside. Remember that Jesus promised, "Whatever you ask for in prayer with faith, you will receive" (Matt. 21:22). He also said, "Ask and it will be given you; search and you will find; knock, and the door will be opened for you." Requests that spring from sincere desire will not go unnoticed.

> *The earliest of prophets and the saints of this millennium have all discovered that the way of faith is not always the way of ease and comfort. Determining to follow Jesus often leads us into paths we would not choose for ourselves. To say yes to God's call requires saying no to our own voice and sometimes to the voices of persons and things we love.*
>
> —Rueben P. Job

Jesus himself gave us the supreme example of the second type of prayer. In the garden he prayed, "Not my will but yours be done." This is a prayer of relinquishment. On the cross Jesus prayed, "Into your hands I commend my spirit" (Luke 23:46). These two forms of prayer on the surface seem to contradict each other. I believe, however, that they are complementary. We desire our deepest needs to be met and our hopes to be fulfilled. But even our most aggressive desires must be surrendered to God, and in the act of surrender we open the door for God to act freely in us. Likely, our soul's deepest desire is born of the Spirit of God. Often this desire is the knowledge of God's will for us, and the prayer of relinquishment becomes at the same time a prayer of affirmation: "Your will be done." Pray for your personal time away.

5. *Make a symbolic sacrifice.* In the spirit of a Lenten commitment, give up something for a few days as a token of your seriousness. Don't make

this a chore. Rather, choose something simple, inconspicuous, and symbolic. For example, consider fasting a meal a day for three days or three meals on one day. Or give up viewing TV for three days prior to your retreat. Some people decide not to drink alcohol as a sign of their sober intention. These gestures remind you of what you will be doing and the weight you are giving to it.

Checklist for Spiritual Preparation
   a. State the purpose of your retreat.
   b. Read before you depart and take along a couple of good books.
   c. Keep a journal both before and during your retreat.
   d. Pray about your retreat daily.
   e. Make a symbolic sacrifice as a reminder to yourself.

Most of these suggestions presume a four- or five-day retreat. Doubtless you can see the value of this groundwork for your fullest experience. But the same principles affect a retreat of a few hours or of a single day. So when you intend to have a brief time away, read over these suggestions and use appropriately in your situation. Whatever the duration of your retreat, it will be enhanced if you have readied yourself. Your retreat begins with your preparation.

I made ready for time with God over the course of a year before going to the desert for a month. Though the retreat's actual duration turned out to be just a little over two weeks, my preparation enabled me to get the most possible from those weeks. From the day I decided to go to the desert and set the date for departure, not a day passed when I did not think about going to the desert to be with God. Preparation played a strong hand in an event that changed the focus of my life and my vocation.

CHAPTER FOUR

CREATING A PLAN
for Your Retreat

....

*Respond to the guidance God gives you on your way
and after you arrive at your place of retreat.*

Like preparation, creating a plan for your time away is another part of the retreat. The plan sketches how you will spend your time, and this picture of the time away begins unconsciously to shape your mind and heart for the experience.

A plan also helps you stay focused. After pondering the reason for making a retreat, the plan outlines an approach to the answer. By evaluating your plan, you can discover whether you are focused on your intention. Staying focused keeps you from wasting time you have set aside to be with God. And if you have discomfort about disturbing your usual routine and facing a day of uncertain activity, creating an outline offers a degree of security. It will identify where you begin and where you will end.

A good retreat generally has some common elements, elements that lie at the heart of a meaningful time with God. For example, silence serves the retreatant well. To be certain you engage your silence, put time for it in the plan.

Your plan likely will include other aspects of any retreat such as bodily and mental stillness, scripture reading, meditation, active listening for God, and reflection on your life.

You will also want to include time with nature, to connect with the earth. A few years ago a friend of mine made a personal retreat to Mepkin Abbey in Moncks Corner, South Carolina. Here he describes how he approached that time: "As I left my room for a stroll, I wondered what God would have me see. So I prayed, 'God, help me to see what you want me to see.' As I walked the gardens I had several "aha!" moments when an ordinary tree or flower or shoreline seemed to be filled with meaning for me. Ever since then, when I'm on retreat and go for a walk, I say, 'God, help me to notice what you want me to see.'"

Each of these rudiments of a retreat provides a way of being with God. Each element can be appropriated to fill a week- or a month-long schedule, but some can also be included even in a half-day retreat. When planning your retreat, include the relevant ways you wish to be with God.

While recognizing all the benefits of creating a plan, remember this caveat: in spite of your forethinking and clear outlining, God may take you a very different way! The paradoxical phrase "wasting time with God" hints at the lack of planning, the loss of goals, and a way that embraces an unstructured, carefree attitude toward the Spirit. No plans! No goals! And no expectations! So I urge you to think about your time away but also to stay open and responsive to the guidance of the Spirit. If you make a plan, you can change the plan. And, if you create a plan, God can override your plan! We humans propose and God disposes. When you have done all you can to prepare yourself and plan your time away, leave it with God and respond to the guidance God gives you on your way and after you arrive at your place of retreat.

Samples of Basic Plans

If you've never made a personal retreat, creating a plan may seem a daunting task. For this reason, and to illustrate a balanced retreat experience, I have developed in outline form a schedule for a retreat of a few hours, an overnight retreat, and a five-day retreat. Alter, adapt, or adjust to fit your unique situation. Try starting with the suggested schedules for your first retreats, and then modify the form based on your needs and the insights derived from your own experience.

A HALF-DAY OR DAY RETREAT

Hold your retreat away from your home if possible. Most people find great value in crossing the threshold between ordinary space and what we may call "desert space." Physically moving from the one to the other space enhances the transition to your retreat. If your retreat will last all day, plan to take two or three books for spiritual reading in the afternoon (see recommendations in the bibliography).

HALF DAY

First Hour

- Become present to your new environment and sit quietly, letting your mind and body get settled in this place. (*15 minutes*)

- Name whatever you are leaving behind. Identify what you are bringing with you to the retreat. Write these reflections in your journal. (*15 minutes*)

- Read a psalm, Pray it. Let the psalm pray you: note how your personal experience connects with the words of the psalmist and the words become your own. Possible psalms to read: 4, 8, 23, or 42.

(Take a short break. Stand, walk, notice your surroundings.)

> *[Nicholas of Cusa] has it that our seeing God consists of our having a sense of God seeing us: to see God is to see one who sees; it is to have an experience of being seen.*
>
> —John S. Dunne

Second Hour

- Choose a biblical text (consider Matt. 6:19-21; 6:22-24; 7:1-5; or 7:7-11). Read the text slowly and reflectively.
- Meditate on the text. Record in your journal how the text touches upon your own life. What in your life does the text bring to your awareness?
- Pray about whatever the text has drawn into your consciousness. Your prayer may be giving thanks, making confession, offering requests, or expressing care for others.
- Turn your consciousness toward God and wait quietly for God to speak. Remember: God's first language is silence.
- Think back over this reading, reflecting, and praying; then record your observations in your journal.

> *"Be silent." Silence frees us from the need to control others. One reason we can hardly bear to remain silent is that it makes us feel so helpless.*
>
> —Richard J. Foster

(Take a 10-minute break. Stretch, walk, notice what is going on with you.)

Third Hour

Follow this comprehensive prayer pattern for an hour of prayer. It is based on W. E. Sangster's "Rule of Prayer" in his book *Teach Me to Pray*.[1] Don't rush. Don't hurry. Delight in your time of conscious communion with God. Take at least three or four minutes with each of the movements. Be slow and deliberate in your prayer.

- Be still. Let both mind and body become quiet. Get seated comfortably. Relax. Take a few deep breaths.
- Remind yourself, *I am on retreat to meet God. No other appointment competes in importance.*
- Adoration. Think on the greatness of God. How incredible it is

that God knows you and desires to have fellowship with you. God is eager to encounter you. Adore God.

- Thanksgiving. Name the things that God has given you for which you are grateful: family, friends, health, work, the church, fun, food, etc. Picture these gracious gifts and thank God for each one.
- Dedication. Review the vows you have taken as a Christian, a church member, a spouse, an employee or employer. Reaffirm these, but also focus intently on what God has brought to your mind this day. Offer your life to God without reserve.
- Guidance. Envision the remainder of your day. Foresee God in each moment, each relationship, each opportunity, each member of your family, and in unscheduled events and encounters. Ask for God's guidance in each aspect of your life.
- Intercession. Make a list of persons who need your prayer. Pray for them by name. Also include in your prayers those whom you love and those who suffer. If we knew what a profound effect our prayer has on others, we would spend more time in prayer. In addition, pray for your country, that the reign of Christ may come in all of our national affairs.
- Petition. Tell God what you most deeply desire in your life. "Whatever you ask for in prayer with faith, you will receive" (Matt. 21:22). Don't be fooled by the blank-check appearance of this promise. As you spend time in God's presence, your desires change; the Spirit crystallizes your true wants. So persist in asking for what you think you really want until you know what it is.
- Act of trust. Intentionally release your prayers to God and trust God to answer them. "Whoever would approach [God] must believe that [God] exists and . . . rewards those who seek [God]" (Heb. 11:6).
- Wait. In the silence wait to hear what God wishes to say to you. "Speak, Lord, your child listens." Repeat the passage for the day and reflect on it. Write it on a slip of paper and carry it with you throughout the day.

A three-hour retreat may end at this point. If you do end here, write a short summary of what happened to you during these three hours of solitude, reflection, and prayer.

FULL-DAY CONTINUATION
Fourth Hour

- Take your meal in silence. Think of yourself as sitting at the table of the Lord; you are eating and drinking in his presence.
- After eating, take a half-hour walk. Use the walk to practice mindfulness. Attend to everything around you: scenery, the earth under your feet, hot sun, or chilly wind. Notice what is going on within you. What are you thinking? What are you feeling?

Fifth Hour

- Look at the books you brought for spiritual reading.
- Browse through these until a passage gets your attention.
- Pause and reflect on the aspect of your life the passage touches.
- Spend the remainder of the hour meditating on each word in the reading. Note in your journal the insights, challenges, and direction that come to you through this reading.

Sixth Hour

- Spend a half-hour freewheeling. Have no agenda; wait before God sitting or standing or walking. Let thoughts come without your effort. Notice their flow and write them in your journal. Let one thought go and welcome the next. No effort. No struggle. Let life come to you and flow through you.
- Transition to departure. Choose a symbolic act, like packing your books or packing your clothes and taking them to the car. This act signals preparation for leaving.
- Keep your journal available. Return to the place, such as the chair in which you sat or amidst the scenery where you walked,

where you have spent most of the day. Make a list of what you are taking home from the retreat.

WHEN PLANS DON'T WORK OUT

AN INTERRUPTED RETREAT

Lalor Cadley is a good friend of mine. She is a retreat leader, a counselor, and a spiritual director. As you will see, she makes careful plans for her retreats, but sometimes they don't work out as scheduled. Learn from her experience!

> I have found that a regular retreat throughout the year makes a great difference in my life. For the last few years I have scheduled four each year. When the new calendars come out, the first thing I do is block out four three-day weekends—in January, April, July, and November—to go off on retreat. I have a simple place that holds me well, a place where I can sink into the silence and tune into the life that's trying to live in me.
>
> I find as I get older that I love the quiet. I used to have to make myself stay still, but lately, much to my surprise, I crave time alone, to rest in God and listen. I'm also, like most people, very busy. Days are scheduled end-to-end, with work and friends and family—all dear to me, and yet it can take all I've got.
>
> This past summer I was set to make my usual trip. My car was in the shop, but I'd found another person going to the same place who said she'd drive me. Then the morning we were scheduled to leave, she called to say there'd been a family crisis and she couldn't go after all.
>
> There I was, packed and ready to go and no way to get there. Now what?
>
> There was a time when I would have turned right back into my regular life. I would have seen those three free days the way a quarterback with the ball sees an open field. Within no time I'd have filled it to the brim. Now I know better. This time wasn't up for grabs. It had been spoken for. I just needed to find

a way to keep my promise, but within the walls of my own house. Surely God was as present here as anywhere.

I unpacked my suitcase, made a cup of tea, and sat down to ponder just how I would go about it. My son was away for the weekend; the pets were at the sitters, so I had the house to myself. I knew if I could be still, what I needed would come to me.

And sure enough, little by little a gentle plan emerged. I offer here some thoughts based on my experience of that weekend, which incidentally was full of grace. I did my best and God was faithful. I offer them not as a prescription but as a stimulant to your own creativity. If you live alone, you're halfway there. For those who live with other people, don't despair. Bring them in on your plan up front. Explain what you want to do and why. You may be surprised to see how willing they are to give you the time and space you need. Especially if they know you're serious.

- Start with prayer. Ask God for the grace to enter into this special time with an open mind and an open heart.
- Create a sacred space in a quiet corner, near a window if possible. Let that be the place where you pray. Find a cloth for the table. Assemble objects that feel sacred—an icon, candle, Bible, photograph, a book of poems, roses, stones. Take your time, and ask God's help in gathering what you need. Don't settle until the space feels right.
- Find music you love that lifts you, whether from Taizé, John Michael Talbot, Anonymous 4, drums and flutes—whatever. Music is a wonderful way to enter into prayer. Put a portable CD player within easy reach of the prayer space.
- Devise a simple rhythm for the day, with the understanding that it can be adjusted in keeping with God's lead. I chose to pray the Liturgy of the Hours morning, midday, and evening (see chapter 5 for an explanation of the hours). This rhythm joins me through Psalms and other scripture with praying Christians all over the world. On this interrupted day, I chose to follow the morning prayer with twenty minutes of silence, breathing deeply, resting in Love.
- Take time after your prayer period for journaling. Record what came to you from your readings, what stirred in you during the silence. You

might also want to record your dreams. The psalmists tell us that God speaks to the beloved in sleep.

- If words are not your medium, try dancing, painting, singing. Be creative. Involve the body, and it will deepen your prayer experience.
- Take a midmorning walk—rain or shine. Notice things: the sound of birds, the smell of earth. Spend time with a flower. Let yourself be awed by the wonders of the world.
- When you feel hungry, enjoy a light lunch, then take a nap or rock yourself to rest, or do some spiritual reading.
- Make time for midday prayer. Return to the Psalms or dip into a favorite prayer book. Let God lead you. Practice *lectio divina* with scripture. Read a passage slowly and notice what draws you. Ask God to guide you as you ponder its meaning for your life.
- Spend time in the afternoon doing manual labor. I learned this practice among the Benedictines, for whom balance is the secret of a holy life. Plant bulbs, split wood, make soup, sweep floors. Whatever you do, go slowly, and be true to the purpose of the work.
- Before supper you might settle down to another twenty-minute period of silence. Centering Prayer is a practice favored by many would-be contemplatives. Don't try to do anything or gain anything. Just be.
- Have a tasty, nourishing supper. Eat slowly. After dinner you may want to continue your spiritual reading or take up a good novel. Write a letter. Strike up a conversation with your guardian angel. Sing to a CD and try to hear what's on your heart.
- Before going to bed, return to the Liturgy of the Hours and pray the evening prayer. Conduct a brief examen (review the day under the eye of God, and answer these two questions: what gave me life today? what drained me?). Go to bed early so you can rise with the dawn and not miss the coming of a new day.
- For those of us who want results, beware. You can be sure this time you give to God will bless you, no matter what does or doesn't happen. Sometimes there are revelations, at other times a quiet comfort. You may be invited to take on a challenge or let go of an illusion. Or it may feel like nothing much has changed. Whatever the outcome, our job is not to evaluate the experience but to have faith in God's promise. Our job is to show up; do what we can to stay present; treat ourselves with great kindness; and trust that at

the deepest level of our being the Indwelling God is hard at work, leading us to life.

When your plans don't work out as you expected, make creative adjustments.

An Overnight Retreat

In outlining an overnight retreat, I envision a person leaving at the end of a regular workday and arriving at the place of retreat before dinner. My suggestions for the first evening are:

- Arrive, unpack, and get settled.
- Get to the retreat mentally and emotionally. Leave behind all work, conflict, worries, and unfinished business. Imagine that you are now on an island, and the drawbridge over which you passed is closed—no way back! Let go of all distractions and leave them behind.
- Eat dinner in silence. Keep your thoughts in the present.
- After dinner, a short walk will help you relax and claim your new space. It will also be a good way to begin examining your heart.
- Before retiring, open your journal and write at the top of a page: "What is going on in my life?" Survey your life and write what comes to you. Consider what is going on at work, with your spouse, your best friends, children, parents, church, and volunteer service. Look more closely at what is going on in your body, your mind (thoughts), emotions, your view of your past, and your opportunities for the future; what is going on between you and God.

In the morning:

- Arise, dress, and ask God's guidance for the day.
- Be prepared to begin your time with God by 9:00 AM.

First Hour

- Review what you wrote in your journal the previous evening.
- Listen to your life. What cries out for attention? What shouts praise and thanksgiving? Where does God seem to be at work in your life at this moment?
- In a relaxed manner muse over these questions. If nothing at first appears, wait, sit still with an openness to the Spirit.
- Make this an unhurried, relaxed time. Be gentle with yourself as you muse over your life.

Remainder of the Day

Follow the suggestions for the full day's retreat as previously outlined.

> *Every prayer-filled day sees a meeting with the God who comes; every night which we faithfully put at his disposal is full of his presence. And his coming and his presence are not only the result of our waiting or a prize for our efforts: they are his decision, based on his love freely poured out.*
>
> —Carlo Carretto

A FIVE-DAY RETREAT

Anticipate arriving in the afternoon or evening to begin your retreat. You may select two, three, or four days from this plan. Each day's plan has continuity, but these days may be changed or rearranged to fit your needs. The design is illustrative, not compulsory. Avoid the attitude that you must work through all the suggestions. Be leisurely. Be gentle with yourself. In a relaxed manner keep yourself engaged with your life, with God, with nature, and with your surroundings. Don't make the retreat another task to complete. The best things that happen on a retreat are often unscheduled. As much as possible, plan to spend your days in silence.

> *All true prayer is based on the conviction of the presence of the Spirit in us and of [the Spirit's] unfailing and continual inspiration. Every prayer in this sense is prayer in the Spirit.*
>
> —Thomas Keating

THE FIRST EVENING

- Get settled in your room.
- Be in touch with the environment where you will be sleeping, resting, and praying.
- Find out what is available to you for reading, relaxing, and reflecting in this particular locale.

THE FIRST DAY

7:45   Read or chant Psalm 10 to set the tone for the day.

8:00   Breakfast

9:00   Engage John 14:1-7 using *lectio divina* as your format. First, read the passage slowly and reflectively. Second, choose the word or phrase that speaks to you and meditate on it; ask what the text is saying to you, what does it call you to do, etc. Third, pray the text—pray about the aspects of your life that the text brings to consciousness. Fourth, cease your activity and "rest in God."

The five exercises for this week originally were created by Julie Johnson and me for the Certificate in Spiritual Formation program at Columbia Theological Seminary in Decatur, Georgia. You will find them most effective when you record and respond to them in writing. Listen to your spirit and push yourself into areas where you are not ready.

10:30 EXERCISE 1: THE TURNING POINTS OF YOUR LIFE
Prepare to write: have paper, pen, and a comfortable place to sit. Enter into silence. Close your eyes, relax, and take several deep breaths—in and out, in and out. The purpose of relaxation and deep breathing is to give you greater access to your deeper self.

Write from this center, this deep inner place of quiet. Be receptive! Write what comes to you. Do not evaluate what you write, do not censor, do not critique or stifle your inspiration in any way. Writing in this manner often takes a little practice. It's okay if you feel a bit stiff or odd. Invite God to be present, protective, and powerful during these writing sessions.

Remember back as far as you can. What do you see or hear? Where were living? What did it look like? Let these images come into your mind.

- Sit in silence for a few minutes.
- Think about the fact that there was a time when you were not—a time when you didn't exist. Then, in God's love, you were created.
- Prayerfully review your life. On your piece of paper draw a vertical line down the left side. At the base of the line, draw a short horizontal mark and write the words: I WAS BORN. Slowly and prayerfully begin to move through the memory of your life.
- Identify the turning points. Say to yourself, "My life was pretty

much the same until
_____."
(Fill in the blank with a word or two.) On your line, make another mark and write a name for this turning point. Slowly review your entire life, naming all the "turning points."

- When you finish, pause for a few minutes. Rest. Notice what your mind goes to. After your pause, review in images the unfolding of your life.

> *[God] comes only through doors that are purposely opened for him. A person may live as near God as the bubble is to the ocean and yet not find him. [God] may be "closer than breathing, nearer than hands or feet," and still be missed.*
>
> —Rufus Jones

Take it easy, go slowly. As you review your life, make note of what comes to you. Write these insights in your journal.

Your life is a gift. Look over the turning points and receive your life with gratitude. Your life is a precious gift from God. You are the sum of all these events, and more!

At the top of a fresh sheet of paper, write the word REFLEC-TIONS. Write answers to the following questions:

What have you discovered in your writing?

(Pause and reflect.)

What did you feel/think as you wrote? as you reflected?

(Pause and reflect.)

What insights into your life came to you?

(Pause and reflect.)

Complete this sentence, "As I look back over my life, God _____" (write as long as anything comes to you).

(Pause and reflect.)

Bring your writing to a close for today.

Close with prayer.

11:30 Take a break.

You have been engaged in hard work, not difficult but energy-consuming. In the time remaining before lunch, take a break, perhaps a short walk or sit in the midst of nature. Choose one of these questions to consider:

1. What recurring themes do you notice in your life?
2. What does your life seem to be about?
3. If you are "a word of God," what is God saying through you?
4. How can you become relaxed and still, so that you may hear God?
5. What do you wonder about in the way your life has unfolded?

12:00 Lunch—Endeavor to maintain your silence. Casual conversation is not of value for a serious retreat.

12:30 Time to read, rest, or nap.

3:30 Reading: Section I of *The God Who Speaks: Learning the Language of Love* (Ben Campbell Johnson, Grand Rapids, MI: Wm. B. Eerdmans, 2004)

6:00 Dinner

7:00 Review the day. Note in your journal the reactions you have had to the retreat thus far. Review this first day and note questions or insights that have come to you. Are there parts of your life that you are having difficulty facing?

THE SECOND DAY

7:45 Read Psalm 42. Let it set the tone for the day.

8:00 Breakfast

9:00 Rewrite 1 Corinthians 13 in your own words. For instance, it might begin, "If I speak with great eloquence and impress others by my rhetoric but I don't have love, my words don't count for anything. If I have the gift of speaking for God but have no love for those to whom I speak, all my insight counts for nothing."

10:00   Take a break.

10:30   EXERCISE 2: THE CHAPTERS OF YOUR LIFE
Take out your journal. Locate the turning points of your life. On a
fresh page in your journal, on the left-hand side, make a second list of
your turning points with a notation of your approximate age when the
event occurred.

Read over this list of occurrences in your life. Visualize where you
were when each took place, how you felt, and how each seems to affect
your life today.

After reviewing your life, think of each space between the turning
points as a chapter in your life. Recall what happened during the
interim periods—moves, sickness, new discoveries, a love affair—and
jot down a list of these happenings between the turning points.

Think of this exercise as preparation for writing an autobiography.
What would you name each chapter based on the things that occurred
and how they affected you?

Take your time. Get a grasp of your life. Or, let your life grasp you.

With all the chapters named, what title for your autobiography do
they suggest? Another way of summing up your life is to ask again,
What is God seeking to say to the world through my life?

When you have finished, take a break until lunch. Again you may
find walking, sitting in the woods or next to a lake or stream, or simply being still allows space to notice what comes to you after this
intense period of work.

12:00   Lunch
 1:00   Time to read, rest, or nap. Optional: Read Section II of *The
        God Who Speaks.*
 3:00   Spend an hour with nature. Walk or find a quiet place to sit.
        Notice carefully the trees, shrubs, birds, and animals. Can you
        feel yourself part of this panorama of God? Bring something
        back from your nature walk to place in your room, such as a
        leaf, limb, or rock. Take the remainder of the afternoon to BE.
 6:00   Dinner—Keep your silence. Let it soak into your soul.

7:00 Reading
8:00 Review the day. Note the thoughts, feelings, and insights that have come to you throughout the day.

THE THIRD DAY

7:45 Read or chant Psalm 130.
8:00 Breakfast
9:00 Bible reading: Mark 2:1-12. Read the story of the healing of the paralytic two or three times until the story is firmly fixed in your mind. Imagine that you are one of the four persons carrying the paralytic to Jesus. Write a first-person account of this healing from the perspective of one of these four persons. Use your imagination. Include what you see, hear, smell, feel, and taste. When you have finished writing, read over the account. What do you learn about yourself in what you have written?
10:00 Take a break.

> *Lord, You know what is most profitable to me: do this or that according to Your will. Give me what You will, as much as You will, and when You will.*
>
> —Thomas à Kempis

10:30 EXERCISE 3: SIGNS OF GRACE AND MOMENTS OF PAIN
In this journaling session you will continue to review your life. Review the turning points and chapter titles that you created in the previous sessions. Add any new turning points that occur to you.

On a clean page in your journal create three columns. Label the first column on the left CHAPTERS. Copy your chapter titles into this column. Take your time and relive these various periods of your life.

Above the second column, write SIGNS OF GRACE. Slowly pray through your life noting the signs of grace. A time of grace may be a person, a place, an event, an encounter with God, a "lucky" coincidence or happening.

Take your time. Write what comes to you. You may not be able to come up with an entry for each chapter. When you finish, put your pen down and muse over what you've written. What do you notice?

Choose one SIGN OF GRACE. Close your eyes. In your imagination look at this person, this event, or this happening and then look through it, like a window, and see God's love for you or God's initiative in your life.

As you sit in God's presence, know that God looks upon you with tenderness and love. These signs of grace bear witness to you of the promises of God for you. These events are a living testimony to God's love and presence in your life.

At the top of the third column, write TIMES OF BROKENNESS AND PAIN. Once again examine your life, and in this column list incidents of brokenness and pain. This might be a personal failure, a loss, a time of confusion or emptiness, a regret, a feeling of guilt or shame, a tragedy, an injury, or an illness.

As you examine times of brokenness and pain, you may notice new signs of grace. If you do, simply write it in the appropriate space. When you have finished, put down your pen and rest. What do you notice about this life review? Do you see any connections between the times of brokenness and the signs of grace?

Choose any chapter of your life containing brokenness and pain except the present one. Consider this chapter and respond to the question *Where was God in this time of brokenness and pain?*

You might try looking at your signs of grace for clues. If you don't see any signs, write about not knowing or seeing any.

Complete this sentence: *In this pain I think that God was seeking to* _____. What would it take to let go of the pain today?

Write a memo to God.

To: God
From: your name
Re: subject

Date:

Begin it this way:

On this day, I relinquish _____. I ask _____. I need _____.

I thank _____. I wonder _____.

12:00 Lunch

 1:00 Time to read, rest, or nap. Optional: Read Section III of *The God Who Speaks.*

 4:00 Take a long walk. Pay special attention to nature. During your walk pick up some object in nature and study it. Look at every side, its shape, marks, meaning, and role in the world.

 6:00 Dinner

 7:00 A brief Bible reading (Psalm 131)

THE FOURTH DAY

 7:45 Read Psalm 121.

 8:00 Breakfast

 9:00 Listen to a text. Read it aloud: Mark 4:3-9. What is this parable about? What does it mean? What does it say to you in your life today? What does it call you to do? How will you respond to the truth that it delivers?

10:00 Take a short break.

10:30 EXERCISE 4: LISTENING TO A CHAPTER OF YOUR LIFE

On a fresh sheet of paper in your journal, draw a horizontal line. At each end of the line draw a short vertical line, forming bookends.

I ⸺⸺⸺⸺⸺⸺⸺⸺⸺⸺⸺⸺⸺ I

Look back over the chapters on your lifeline. Pause at each chapter. Move deliberately. Permit a chapter to choose you for further exploration. Prayerfully discern which chapter "chooses" you and write the name of that chapter between the bookends. Write the turning point that begins this chapter underneath the left bookend. Write the turning point that ends the chapter underneath the bookend on the right.

Below the chapter title and the bookends, write: "It was a time when . . . ." Answer each of the following questions beginning with that phrase, "It was a time when. . . ."

> *Prayer, as the distilled awareness of our whole life before God, is meant to lead us to a radical transformation of consciousness in which all of life becomes a symbol. All of life is seen as God sees it.*
>
> —James Finley

What was going on in the world that affected you? What years were these? What was being reported in the newspaper and on television?

What was happening in the nation at this time? at work or school or your neighborhood?

What was going on in your family? your immediate family? your extended family?

Who claimed your attention during this period?

    spouse or siblings?

    friends?

    coworkers?

    neighbors?

    an antagonist?

    no one?

What was going on with you?

    physically?

    emotionally?

What were you thinking and feeling about yourself in these days?

What was occurring in your spiritual life?

What was happening between you and God?

How did this time affect your faith?

Is there one event that stands out above the others?

    perhaps a turning point?

    a crisis?

    a revelation?

    an awareness?

    a decision?

Pause for a bit. Muse over what you have written. After reviewing this chapter of your life, take time to complete this sentence again: "It was a time when . . . ."

Using your imagination, find a metaphor or symbol that best captures the essence of this chapter. For example: *This time was like*:

- a whirlwind
- a hidden meadow
- a newborn baby
- a dark storm
- a wounded soldier
- a rainbow

What symbol comes to your mind? Now try something a little different. Move more into the creative side of your brain. Try doodling or drawing your metaphor or symbol. You will not be laughed at or graded. No one will see this. Just try drawing or doodling a little.

Finally, I invite you to write out a conversation with the symbol or metaphor you've chosen. Maybe five or six exchanges back and forth, at least.

One way to begin would be:

Ben: *What are you trying to say to me?*

Symbol:

Ben:

When you finish your dialogue with the symbol, write a closing prayer. Bring all you have thought and felt and discovered before God. (If you thought the dialogue with a symbol was stupid or silly, go back and do it! It holds greater possibility than you can imagine.)

12:00	Lunch
1:00	This is a time to let your life float. Pay attention to the ideas that come to you. Listen to the yearning of your heart. Reject nothing that seeks to claim your attention.
4:30	Write a letter to your spouse or to your best friend explaining what you are experiencing. You may not mail it or give it to the person, but it will be meaningful to write it.
6:00	Dinner
7:00	Take a walk. Let your mind slip into neutral.
8:30	Review the day. What has inspired you today? What has been your deepest insight for the day? What is your request of God as you come toward the end of your desert experience?

THE FIFTH DAY

7:45	Read or chant Psalm 46.
8:00	Breakfast
9:00	Bible reading: 1 Samuel 3:1-12. Who are the main characters in this text? What role does each play? How is your experience of retreat like Samuel's experience? Who is your Eli? What do you learn from Samuel's example?
10:00	Break

10:30   EXERCISE 5: GUIDANCE FROM FRIENDS

Identify a current issue in the present chapter of your life about which you must make a decision. On a new page in your journal, write a question that drives to the heart of the issue. Examples: *What should I do about . . . ? How shall I deal with . . . ? What changes is God calling me to make about this pressing issue? What is God calling me to do?* Describe the context in which this issue arises.

After defining the issue, look back over your life using the turning points as a guide. Notice the important people in each chapter. Which of these are wisdom figures for you?

Looking back through your memory is like viewing an old photo album. Jot down the names of the people who have been important or significant for you. These may be thought of as wise people, wisdom figures. As you list these persons, be aware of the feelings and thoughts that arise. Don't block them; simply jot down a word or two or offer them to God.

Review your list and place an asterisk next to those who have been spiritually significant to you:

- touchstone people
- wise and loving individuals
- your safe friends and special mentors

These special people are your spiritual family of origin. They are the people who showed you God's love, Christ's forgiveness, and the Spirit's comfort.

Create a Spiritual Family Portrait by drawing a circle with your name in the center. Now write the names of the most significant persons around your name (perhaps four or five names). More than likely, these folks have never been together for a picture. When you are finished, put your pen down and rest. Say a prayer for each person, expressing what each means to you.

Reread the question you wrote when at the beginning of this exercise. Now prayerfully choose someone in your spiritual family with whom to imagine a conversation about your issue. It is best to choose someone with whom you do not have contact currently. The person may be dead, or he or she might be a mentor through writing. Enter into a dialogue with this person about the question in need of discernment. You might start this way:

> *God wants everyone to know God's will. God doesn't withhold grace, play games, or tease us to test our faithfulness or our worthiness to be trusted with divine insight. I am convinced that God is far more prone to human revelation than I am to divine encounter.*
>
> —Danny E. Morris

Me: You are so important to me . . .
Friend:
Me: I need someone to talk to about . . .

Try writing ten or so exchanges.

What insight did you receive? What help with your issue came to you from reflecting, writing, and reviewing?

12:00 Lunch

1:00 Writing a Rule of Life
A retreat is a very fine renewing experience, but your connection with God needs to be nurtured on a regular basis. In a brief outline, list what you will do each day to keep alive your sense of God. What spiritual practices will you incorporate in your life? What will you do each week, each month, and each year? Writing your intentions and asking someone to help you be accountable will strengthen your resolve.

> *Because God often reveals part of the picture to one person and another part to another person, it is prudent to consult one another to discern God's counsel, guidance, and direction, even if there is no apparent reason to do so.*
>
> —Suzanne Farnham

2:00 Make a list of what you are leaving at the retreat site—perhaps fear, anxiety, and disobedience. Also take time to identify what you are taking home with you that will make a difference in your life.

3:00 Have a safe journey home. "Go with God."

After you return home, review the suggestions concerning reentry found in chapter 7.

CHAPTER FIVE

Retreat at a Monastery

....

You are choosing to immerse yourself
in a rhythm of daily prayer.

What do you do on a retreat? Some years ago a friend of mine came to town unexpectedly, arriving on a day I had set aside for time away on retreat. I invited him to join me.

In the fall of 1999 I was a guest of a monastery for the first time. I made my way to a weeklong visit for study and prayer feeling both excited and nervous. Knowing almost nothing about monastic life, I was uncertain whether I would like the frequent hours of prayer and the commitment to silence that would be a part of the experience. I did not realize that my encounter with the Cistercian monks would be the beginning of a new and significant journey of faith for me.

As soon as I arrived, I began to be glad. The men and women who live in monastic communities take seriously the scriptural instruction to be gracious hosts. Because they expect to meet the risen Lord in their encounter with "strangers," they receive visitors with a warmth and grace unusual in our world. The guest master met me as I checked in, made sure I knew where and when the next worship would be, and

THIS CHAPTER IS BY PAUL H. LANG.

then led me to my simple, clean room. That evening the abbot and guest master provided a brief period of instruction for the guests.

Going to the monastery is different from going to church camp or a conference center in several ways. When you go to a monastery, you will be a part of an ongoing community. The brothers or sisters with whom you eat, work, and pray have committed themselves to a specific kind of life—a life that may seem archaic and countercultural to us. At the heart of the life of the monastery is the discipline of praying the Daily Offices (sometimes called the Liturgy of the Hours or Breviary). This discipline requires the community to gather for regular daily times of prayer; silence and work are woven in between prayer. Typically, though the number is determined by each monastery, there are between four and eight periods of prayer, beginning in the early morning and ending in late evening. When you make a monastic retreat, you will be choosing to immerse yourself in this rhythm of daily prayer as a core practice. There are many different monastic traditions in Christendom. Each has wonderful lessons to teach you as a guest. In what follows I will be describing the experience you would expect at a monastic community shaped by the Benedictine tradition, but much of what I describe will be descriptive of other monastic traditions too.

Preparation for a Monastic Retreat

Preparing for a monastic retreat, as for any personal retreat, will assure a more meaningful experience. Let me begin by clarifying several points: first, the words *monastery* and *monk* are both gender-neutral terms and refer both to men and women. Second, my suggestions for preparation are equally applicable for planning a retreat in a monastery or convent. Finally, men are often welcome as guests in female monastic communities, and women are often welcomed as guest at male monastic communities. When you call to make reservations you can check to confirm this. Speak with the person who schedules guest accommodations. You may be able to secure a room on short notice, but it is better to make reservations well in advance. Each monastic community has different types of accommodations for guests, so find out what the options are when you call. If you have specific dietary or mobility restrictions, bring up those specific needs when you make your reservation. Most monasteries serve healthy and tasteful food at a reasonable cost, and the dietician can make allowances for dietary restrictions.

If you are making your first monastic retreat, or you are visiting a new community with which you are unfamiliar, ask the guest master to schedule a time to help you become oriented to the schedule, facilities, and patterns of life in the monastery. This will not take a long time, and it will help you feel at ease with your new surroundings.

Life in the Monastery

Since the beginning of the Christian church there have been people who felt a call to "pray without ceasing" as scripture instructs. In the fourth century men and women left society and lived in isolation in the desert, devoting themselves to a life of unceasing prayer. In some cases people followed them and lived nearby in order to receive instruction and encouragement in living a life devoted to God .

These fathers and mothers (abbas and ammas) of the desert became devout, compassionate, and wise. People sought them out for their compassion and counsel. But not all people could withstand the rigors of isolation in the desert. Over time, some began to live in communities in which they could offer more substantial support and instruction to one another as they grew in their practice of prayer. They formulated rules to govern their common life. In the sixth century, Saint Benedict of Nursia created a rule to govern his community. Benedict's Rule has had a pervasive influence in the development of monastic communities in the West. Indeed, Benedict is often called the "Father of Western Monasticism."

The Rule of Saint Benedict instructs the community to live a balanced life of work, prayer, and rest. While individual growth in holiness is important, the community's growth in holiness is paramount. People are to spend daily time alone with God, but they are also expected to live in and contribute to the community. Silence is kept as

Resources for Finding a Monastic Community

Author Karen Sloan (*Flirting with Monasticism*, InterVarsity Press, 2006) has a Web page of annotated links to monastic communities. http://karensloan.net/monastic/links/

My first monastic visit was to Monastery of the Holy Spirit in Conyers, Georgia, and I still think of this monastery as "home." http://www.trappist.net/

The Order of Saint Benedict (OSB) has a well-developed Web site which includes links to Benedictine retreat houses both within the USA and international ones as well. http://www.osb.org/retreats/index.html

The Order of Presbyterian Benedictines has a small but growing list of communities linked on its site. Members have found meaningful opportunities for study and retreat in these places. http://www.presbenedict.org/Order_of_Presbyterian_Benedictines/Links.html

a way to provide an atmosphere of solitude with God while living in community. Silence encourages deep communion with God by preventing the constant interruptions of idle chatter. Further, the pace of life in a monastic community is more relaxed and orderly than the pace many people live. You may need a day or so to slow down and immerse yourself in the experience of being with God and with the members of in the monastic community.

In most monastic settings you'll find simple and healthy meals. Typically, meals are eaten in silence, or someone reads from scripture or the writings of the church during the meal. In some monasteries a "talking" area for dining is available also.

You may find that the monastery provides spiritual guidance through the counsel of one of the brothers or sisters. You can inquire about this with the guest master or director of hospitality, who will schedule a time for you to speak with the spiritual guide.

Most monasteries have ongoing work of some sort to help sustain the community financially. If you want to participate completely in the life of the monastery, you can inquire about opportunities to work during the time between the Daily Offices. This work can be as simple as washing the dishes or as exotic as working with stained glass or bonsai. The work opportunities will vary at each setting.

"Off time" can also be spent simply resting in your room, walking the grounds, praying in the sanctuary/chapel, reading, or writing. Whatever you choose to do with the off hours, I encourage you not to leave the monastery. Do not go shopping or to the movies, for example. The retreat at a monastery should be an uninterrupted block of time in which you are consciously open to the work of God. During the retreat you will adopt a new pace for life and new activities to fill your day. So commit yourself to staying at the monastery and fully experiencing the life offered to you in that setting. You don't have to understand fully or even appreciate the reasons for this pattern of life in order to live it faithfully for a few days or a week. If that means getting up to pray at 3:00 or 4:00 AM each day, do it and discover how prized those early morning prayers can become.

In the monastery there is a hallowing of time. By that I mean that God is sought and cherished in each moment. Prayer punctuates and infuses each day. The rhythm and pace of each day are designed to enhance the experience of the holy. Time spent in a monastery will be divided between corporate worship, time for work, time alone with God in silence, and time to rest. Often the guest master will offer instruction about some spiritual discipline or about the monastic life.

THE DAILY OFFICE

Worship is organized into seven daily times of prayer. Each of these times of prayer is assigned a particular time of day and has a particular quality to it. These Daily Offices, as they are called, are a tool to aid the community in remaining aware of the presence of God throughout the day. Singing the Psalms is the common thread in these times of prayer. All one hundred and fifty psalms are sung in a carefully ordered pattern, which typically cycles every two weeks. Imagine! The monks and nuns sing all one hundred and fifty psalms twenty-six times in a single year. Different communities may sing through the Psalms on a more or less frequent cycle, as their circumstance requires.

Praying the Daily Offices is at the heart of a monastic retreat. As mentioned above, these frequent periods of prayer aid in the hallowing of time. Each office contributes a unique movement on the daily pilgrimage of faith. Together, the seven offices "move" through a journey of faith. On a miniature scale this movement parallels the journey of our entire life of faith. Further, the Daily Offices will take you on a journey through the week, the liturgical seasons, and (if you keep them over time) the Christian year. I have been praying the offices for several years now. This is the journey I make each day as I pray them:

VIGILS [in darkness at 4:00 AM]
I wake to search for and wait for God. I ask myself during the extended time of silence, *How can my life in the day ahead cooperate with the work that God has already begun?* (After vigils I go back to bed and sleep until lauds.)

LAUDS [sunrise]
I praise God for God's faithfulness in offering me unmerited love. In gratitude for that amazing grace I offer myself and my labors of the day in service to God.

TERCE [midmorning]
I touch base with God. By 9:00 AM I have new "material" from my life to pray about: people for whom I wish to intercede, others I need to forgive, and words and deeds of my own in need of forgiveness. I ponder the arrival of the Holy Spirit at Pentecost at the third hour and wait, hoping for the Spirit to arrive and direct me in faithfulness.

SEXT [midday]

This is my midday time out. I stop, take stock of what I've done and need to do. I ponder the crucifixion and confess to God the sins from my own life that hurt God and God's people. I rededicate the remainder of the day to God in loving service.

NONE [midafternoon]

An afternoon time to touch base again with God. I ponder Peter's role in helping to heal the man with the crippled hand and ask, *Whose healing can I be a part of today if I would make time to show compassion and be with them?* I consider Jesus dying, forsaken on the cross, and let that bring to my attention those people in the world who also are isolated and who are suffering.

VESPERS [sunset]

I am grateful. Gratitude is the hallmark of deep love for God, and vespers is the time when I feel and express that gratitude most fervently. I am grateful for light and life, for work to do, for family and friends who love me, for the gifts of grace that rain down around me, and for the times I met Christ during my day.

COMPLINE [before retiring]

I seek and prepare for "a restful night and peace at the last." I set aside my worries and concerns, entrusting them to God's safekeeping and I remind myself of my baptismal identity. In life and in death, I belong to God.

THE ORDERING OF TIME

How time is organized can tell us a lot about what a community believes and values. In a monastic community, time is organized around the Daily Offices. But knowing that the Divine Office is central only gives us a partial appreciation for the many subtle layers of meaning that the organization of time in a monastery will teach us. For example, remember that the goal is to come to a place where prayer is unceasing. Though the seven Daily Offices provide a structured way to grow toward the goal of unceasing prayer, they are merely a tool toward that end.

Look at time from several vantage points in order to discern some of the overlapping meanings which time, if we are observant, teaches us.

- God is Lord of all time—past, present, and future. In the monastery you will conclude nearly every psalm with the words "Glory be to the Father and to the Son and to the Holy Spirit. The God who is, who was, and is to come at the end of the ages." This doxology reminds us that our past, our present, and our future all reside within God's time.

- Each moment is considered a likely time for an encounter with God. In a life of unceasing prayer, we are constantly aware of God with us.

- Each day offers clues to growing into a life of prayer. The Daily Offices follow the Hebrew pattern for "day" that Jesus and his disciples knew and that the early Christian church inherited. In the Hebrew tradition, the day begins with sunset (think of Genesis where God's work of creation is punctuated by the narrator's observation of the passing of each day: "There was evening and there was morning . . ."). One lesson this tradition might hold is that we begin the "work" of our day best when we start by surrendering our will to God. Then, when we arise early in the morning, we imagine that God has already been "at work" for hours while we slept. Our task is to join God in the work already begun.

- In the Liturgy of the Hours, the days of the week are influenced by the preceding Sunday. For example, the Daily Offices in the week that follows the First Sunday of Advent will be built around the themes and scripture passages that correspond to the season of Advent. The same will be true for other Sundays, particularly those Sundays that mark a significant festival or a theologically weighty celebration—like Reign of Christ, Epiphany, or Pentecost Sundays.

- To a lesser degree, days within each week will have theological connections to biblical passages and themes independent of the Sunday that precedes them. For example, Sundays may emphasize the events of the triumphal entry into Jerusalem, the day of resurrection, or one of the postresurrection appearances. Wednesdays have a long history of being a day of penitence and fasting. On Thursdays you may find the liturgy alluding to events of Maundy Thursday in Holy Week, and to the final discourse of Jesus to the disciples. Like Wednesday, Friday traditionally has been a penitential day focused on the events of the Passion. Saturday, the sabbath day, emphasizes the need to ebb and flow in rest and work. Saturday also includes the hopeful anticipation of Holy Saturday (Easter eve), and often expressed in the prayers and songs of Saturday offices.

SILENCE

Life and worship in a monastery allow for frequent periods of silence. Learning to appreciate the space that the silence provides is a key component for entering into a monastic retreat. Let the periods of silence, which slow the pace of worship, be a respite from and an antidote for the excessive busyness and frenzied nature of modern life. Enter deeply into the silence before, during, and after the worship. A few ideas may suggest how to engage and use the silence more effectively:

> *I know that in the silence of my heart you will speak to me and show me your love. Give me, O Lord, that silence. Let me be patient and grow slowly into this silence in which I can be with you. Amen.*
>
> —Henri J. M. Nouwen

- Sit erect, breathe deeply,
  follow your breath inward, and relax.

- In the silent space between chanting the Psalms, reflect on your experience.
- You may focus on a word or phrase from the scripture that was meaningful.
- When your mind wanders, be gentle with yourself. Draw it back.
- Try repeating the phrase *Be still, and know that I am God.*
- Pray the Lord's Prayer in silence. Each time your mind wanders, begin again at the beginning. (For more on silence, see chapter 6.)

SINGING

Singing is an essential aspect of monastic worship that grows out of chanting the Psalms. Unlike other portions of scripture, which may have existed in spoken or written form before they were set to music, the Psalms have no history apart from the history of being sung. Indeed, we believe that they were being sung for a long time before they were written. Christians have preserved the Jewish practice of singing the Psalms and continue to sing the Psalms today.

> *Hidden away deep within my heart was a loving being named God who would always love me and would never leave me. It was at this time that a wise teacher taught me about friendship with God.*
>
> —Joyce Rupp

When singing the Psalms, let your singing reflect the disposition of your heart, which the worship shapes even as you sing. As Benedict instructs, "Mind and voice must be in harmony." If you find the emotions of a particular psalm you are singing to be alien to your experience, then imagine that they represent the feelings and experiences of others in the community who need to find the expressions of their life in scripture.

In his *Confessions*, Augustine described the effect of singing in worship: "How much did I weep during hymns and verses, greatly moved at the sweet singing of thy Church. Their sounds would penetrate my ears and their truth melt my heart, sentiments of piety would well up, tears would flow and that was good for me."[1] As you sing, let the disposition of your heart be informed by the content of the scripture, psalms, prayers, and hymns. Let the words and the music move you deeply and take you to an authentic encounter with God.

In general, you want to sing the Psalms in a gentle, even voice, in a way that emphasizes the communal nature of the chanted Psalm. That is a nice way of saying, "Don't sing too loudly!" A good way to be sure you are singing in ensemble with the others is to ask yourself, *Can I hear the others singing?* and, *Is my voice blending along with theirs to form one voice of the whole group?* The texture of chanted psalms is exquisite when everyone is singing with one voice. Relax. Sing in a way that is as much listening as making music, and find the tempo that the psalm will give to you if you are sensitive to it.

Also, when a group of people sings the Psalms, two subgroups usually form to sing the Psalms in an antiphonal pattern. That is, group A will sing a portion of the psalm and then sit silently while group B sings the next portion of the psalm. Many find a calming beauty in the ebb and flow of singing the Psalms antiphonally.

Finally, there are portions of the singing that are given specifically to one person, typically the music leader, who is called the cantor or "hebdomadary." Sometimes the cantor will sing the verses of the psalm while the other worshipers sing various responses or refrains. It is also typical for the cantor to sing the first cadence of every psalm as a solo. Then the other worshipers join the cantor after he or she has established the pitch and tempo of the music. Do not compete with your cantor. Sing gently enough that you can hear him or her and follow the cantor's lead.

Glossary of Terms

Literature describing the Liturgy of the Hours or the Divine Office will often use unfamiliar terms to the first-time visitor. This glossary introduces frequently used words and their meaning.

Antiphon. A portion of a psalm, lifted out and sung at the start and conclusion of the psalm. This portion is selected for the extra repetition because it helps to make the psalm a personal prayer; the phrase warrants additional attention because of its centrality to the meaning of the psalm; or it lifts up themes relevant to the office being sung.

Antiphonal. The practice of singing short portions of a psalm text in an alternating pattern between groups.

Canticle. A song from scripture. From Latin *canticulum*, "little song." We find these throughout scripture. Some are assigned to specific offices.

Cantor. Music leader. From Latin *canere*, "sing."

Collect. A prayer that reflects on the psalm or scripture just read or sung, or which explores or expands upon the themes of the office or liturgical season. The formal Collect prayer includes five distinct parts: (1) Naming God, (2) Naming a Divine Attribute, something God is or does, (3) Making Supplication—asking God to act on our (or others') behalf in a way consistent with the attribute given before, (4) The Implication—describing the results of God's action, (5) The Signature—usually a Trinitarian conclusion.

Eucharist. The Sacrament of Holy Communion, or The Lord's Supper. A name for the sacrament that emphasizes thanksgiving. From Anglo-French *eukariste*, based on Greek *eu*, "well" + *charizesthai*, "offer grace." The sacrament that reminds us of God's amazing grace and our grateful opportunity to respond.

Hebdomadary. A person assigned to be liturgist for a given week. From Latin *hebdomadalis*, "lasting seven days," and Greek *hebdomas*, "seven days."

Invitatory. An exhortation to praise God. The office of Vigils each day begins with an Invitatory Psalm. The Invitatory Psalms historically have been limited to Psalms 24, 67, 95, and 100.

Magnificat. The Song of Mary found in Luke 1:46-55. From Latin *magnificat*, "magnifies," the first word of the passage in Latin.

Nunc Dimittis. The Song of Simeon found in Luke 2:29-32. From Latin "(Lord), now let (your servant) depart," which begins the passage.

Office(s). Also called the Divine Offices, Daily Offices, Liturgy of the Hours, or the Breviary. From Latin *opus*, "work," and *facere*, "do." Benedict describes praying of the offices as doing the "work of God." Though actual practice varies from community to community, the offices consist of seven daily times of prayer (Psalm 119:164) that are performed at roughly the following times.

Vigils	4:00 AM (or in some traditions, midnight)
Lauds	sunrise (the "first" hour)
Terce	9:00 AM (originally three hours from the "first" hour)
Sext	12:00 noon (originally six hours from the "first" hour)
None	3:00 PM (originally nine hours from the "first" hour; sometimes the "little hours" of Terce, Sext, and None, are collapsed into a single office, Prayers at Midday.)
Vespers	sunset
Compline	8:00 or 9:00 PM, at the close of the day

INVITATION TO A MONASTIC RETREAT

A friend participated in a week-long retreat at a Benedictine monastery in the desert. In a few words he endeavored to capture the meaning of this experience for himself and for others who might share the experience. He wrote the following letter to a couple of friends to encourage them to make a retreat at the monastery he visited.

Read this letter as if it were written to you, encouraging you to make a similar retreat.

Like many Benedictine monasteries, Christ in the Desert is designed to afford guests of "all flavors" a quiet, beautiful-beyond-belief place to stay. The cost is reasonable. They have a number of guesthouses. Couples can stay together in several of the double rooms.

The location of the monastery is off the charts, lovely beyond description, about fifteen miles off the highway above Abiquiu, New Mexico.

The monks keep the Hours, just as Benedictines have for over a thousand years. So they have seven services during the day, beginning at 4:30 AM (Vigils) and ending at 9:30 PM (Compline).

Guests are invited to attend. The monks sit on two sides of the chapel and chant the Psalms, back and forth, in amazingly beautiful plainsong. Guests are seated at the back of the chapel on left and right sides and are invited to sing along with the monks on their side of the chapel. Booklets are provided with very simple script, which I found easy to read, guiding guests in the chanting. We all loved it.

Guests share meals with the monks in silence, in a large room. Food is good. Monks sit on one side and guests on the other. This too is quite an experience!

Think about it. I guarantee you that this is an experience that you will never forget!

If you want to spend some time here, you should e-mail the monastery soon, to see if they have room.

Steve

CHAPTER SIX

Entering the Silence

This Great Silence, possessing an energy and power of its own, operates in profound levels of the soul; it is far from neutral because it exerts power and precipitates change.

At the Monastery of the Holy Spirit in Conyers, Georgia, Father Girard, the guest master, gathered all the retreatants in the conference room. On a table in the middle of the room he placed a three-gallon jar filled with muddy, murky water. He then began to speak about the life of the monastery—the rules for talking, eating, praying. He went on to suggest what could aid us in our time away from busy lives, seeking quiet and solitude. As he spoke, I glanced at the jar of muddy water; it had begun to clear up. The sediment had settled, and the water was becoming transparent. Without calling attention to his object lesson, Father Girard had illustrated what silence could do with the murkiness of our lives. Be still, be quiet. The sediment in your life will settle, and your mind and spirit will become clear.

Many of us have lived with noise so long that we have no idea where the path of silence lies. I read of a woman preparing to go on a silent retreat who packed mail that had accumulated on her desk, a bit of transcription work to complete, and her TV/DVD player. When she arrived at the retreat site with all her stuff, a friend asked, "What is it about the words 'silent retreat' that you don't understand?" We sympathize with this woman because we too have sought hard to find the rich and promising land of silence but remain captive to our distractions.

In the unfolding of my life, I have often wondered whether I would ever find a place of inner peace, of rest and quiet. Often I frankly doubted I could come to such a place, but "Something" in me refused to let me live in turmoil; a Geiger counter of the soul clicked when noise and confusion got beyond endurance. Repeatedly this peace sensor reminded me inner quiet is possible. It kept my hope alive.

Let me tell you about my journey into silence, that is, into as much silence as I have discovered. I had been a Christian believer for two decades before the notion of silence ever came to me. Like many of my contemporaries, I lived as though nothing was happening between God and me unless I was talking either mentally or out loud.

My first feeble efforts at discovering the silence were inspired by a secular book on meditation. The author described ways to relax the body, empty it of tension, and focus on the silence within. He wrote extensively about breathing, how the breath could serve to quiet the spirit. I sometimes felt touched by the silence, but I found it difficult to take the inner quiet of meditation into the hurly-burly of daily life.

In my quest for quiet, both within and without, I have found that place can make a huge contribution to the search. For me, the places conducive to finding silence largely have been Catholic monasteries, where monks pray seven times daily. Perhaps it is my imagination, but I find that driving onto the grounds of the monastery at Conyers, Georgia, brings me peace and a sense of God's presence. When I go to the monastery for a day or two, I find new ways to "waste time with God," to slip my gears into neutral, to let go of everything and settle into a deep silence.

For the past few years I have been on a serious journey into silence. I have committed to a daily period of quiet and personal retreats where I engage the silence. Wandering thoughts still distract me; ideas stimulate my mind and draw me away from the silence; my imagination can also be an enemy on the journey into silence. Sometimes when least expected, my soul is touched by the silence. The still, placid lake nestled in the mountains depicts this silence. Like the lake, the silence lies still—no wind, no wave, nothing to mar its mirror-like reflection. The silence lets me ease into the water, give myself to its warmth and buoyancy; it will hold me, sustain me, and refresh me. I relax, not fighting the water. Instead, I go with it, give myself to it, and let it hold me. I permit the silence to take me farther and farther out of myself.

This Great Silence, possessing an energy and power of its own, operates in profound levels of the soul; it is far from neutral because it exerts power and precipitates change. Maybe someday I will know this Silence well enough to express it more clearly. When the Great Silence penetrates my spirit, it seems to me that I experience momentary unity with God.

Having had my own struggles with coming to quiet, I found a dear friend's account of her own experience quite humorous. Here she describes groping for inner stillness, raising the kind of questions that get settled after one or two retreats. Notice how her mind bounces from one image to another.

> I went into the silence
> Intentionally
> but also warily.
> It was worse than I imagined
>   and better.
> Once a day or twice,
> I'd walk down the small road to nowhere
> trying to pick up a cell phone signal.
> Thankfully, every time I called home
>   my husband picked up the phone.
>   Wow, he sounded great,
>   and generally he seemed glad to hear from me,
>   amused at my daily escapes from the silence.
>
> Who are these people who live in silence?
> Are these leaders married?

I think so. They have matching wedding bands.
She was raised Methodist,
and both of them are graduates of seminary.
But he dons a cassock for evening prayer,
        and there are so many statues of Mary around here.
Is he Catholic? Did he leave the priesthood to get married?
        Or, is he just a very high-church Methodist? . . .

Funny how your mind hiccups in S I L E N C E!
What is this enforced silence at meals?
Is it a way to avoid the mindless chatter that can fill the
mealtime?
In some ways it relieves me of responsibility.
        But I also feel like I'm missing something by not
knowing my table companions.
        This is a different sort of hospitality—the priest
reading as we are gathered for a meal, avoiding all eye contact,
        And soon I joined those who pick up a book and
stay unto themselves. . . .
Did Jesus have silent meals?
        Even with Zacchaeus or Mary and Martha?
Twice I nearly said, "Thank you for the delicious meal."
        Imagine! I nearly laughed out loud when I caught
myself about to speak. Nearly laughed out loud! Oh, my.
        Tonight I completely entertained myself through the
entire meal by imagining myself talking during the meal
        and how they would quiet me.
Of course, it is amazing to watch their nonverbal hospitality,
        Knowing just when to pass a dish, etc.
Do they talk when retreatants are not present?
Tonight with only a friend present, there was a whisper or
two. I didn't like it.
Even two or three words seemed to open up possibilities I
did not want. I was the first to leave the table.
I think I heard them twittering among themselves.
Glad I was out of there.
Maybe I relish the silence more than I realized. . . .

I've done a lot of writing on this retreat.
Is it a way of talking to myself or listening for God?
I should do this more often.

Of course, the point of the silence is to listen.
I came to listen.
Thankfully, I am hearing
     mostly through scripture
     and through the sunrise and sunset,
through the taste of the healthy food (served in small dishes
on small plates),
through the lovely candles and weavings and plants and
incense
and the quiet music at worship. . . .
I am hearing my heart beat.
I am hearing again,
and I want to make sure I find ways to stay listening,
so I won't have to come back to a silent retreat any time
soon.

The Need for Silence

We need to find times and places of silence because every day our ears are
bombarded with noise; it's everywhere! From the moment we awaken in
the morning until our head hits the pillow at night, we are assaulted by
noise—traffic, leaf blowers, Muzak. Restaurants too can be filled with the
buzz of waiters dropping glasses, children crying, and people who speak
exceptionally loudly. These references to external noise do not touch the
noise within, which may be louder than the noise on the street. Those
around us cannot hear our inner voices, but we hear them, and they take
their toll on our creativity, productivity, and peace.

In this cacophony of noise, there is one sound that we rarely hear:
the sound of silence. A world without things going on would be awful,
and when things go on noise is inevitable; as a consequence, we must
search for pockets of silence to find respite. Daily those of us who treasure silence engage in a war on noise and, unfortunately, we lose many

battles. Why is that? Are we bored with life? bored with ourselves? Must we be distracted every minute of the day?

In this turbulence we need to find a place of silence where we can receive new strength and discover the Reality that waits for us beyond the noise and distractions of life. What a difference it would make if we could for once stop to explore the depth of silence within us.

The Hebrew and Christian scriptures have commended silence for thousands of years. We hear the invitation to silence both in the directives of scripture and in the examples of believers. These texts offer examples:

> Be still, and know that I am God!—Psalm 46:10

> In the morning, while it was still very dark, he got up and went out to a deserted place, and there he prayed.—Mark 1:35; see Luke 4:42

> For God alone my soul waits in silence;
> from him comes my salvation.
> [God] alone is my rock and my salvation,
> my fortress; I shall never be shaken.—Psalm 62:1-2

> I will meditate on all your work,
> and muse on your mighty deeds. —Psalm 77:12

> Let the words of my mouth and the meditation of my heart
> be acceptable to you,
> O Lord, my rock and my redeemer.—Psalm 19:14

The Meaning of Silence

The silence we seek is more than absence of noise; silence is a deep stillness, a unity of consciousness that gives focus; true silence touches every aspect of life—body, soul, spirit. Then, deeper yet, is the Great Silence.

The Hebrew scriptures begin with the words "In the beginning when God created . . ." (Gen. 1:1). After this opening, the narrative continues with "Then God said, 'Let there be light' . . . 'Let there be . . .' 'Let there be . . .'" until the whole of creation is finished. Between "in the beginning" and "God created" there is a blank, an emptiness—silence if you will! The Great Silence refers to that silence before God's creative speech; it is the Silence of Eternity, the space where God dwells. Romano Guardini, a Roman Catholic priest and scholar, urges us toward this silence when he says that "stillness is the tranquility of the inner life; the quiet at the depths of its hidden stream. It is a collected, total presence, a being 'all there,' receptive, alert, ready." It is when the soul abandons "the restlessness of purposeful activity."[1] Do you see that silence transcends the absence of noise? that it is an interior stillness? It implies restfulness. It signifies a resting place at high noon—placid, peaceful, and cool. Silence is like a safe haven protecting us against the noise that beats on our senses and breaks us down.

Two Types of Silence

In the long history of prayer, those who have gone before us describe two kinds of silence: *kataphatic* and *apophatic*—active and passive prayer. A kataphatic form of prayer relies on images to mediate the presence of God. For example, the pray-er reads the stories of Jesus and with her imagination enters into the biblical world. All the senses are put to use—the smell of the air, the feeling of the warmth of the sun, the sense of sight darkened by the clouds, the taste of the dust and the chirping of a bird.

This form of prayer requires using the imagination. We read, relax, imagine, and attend feelings and desires. We are indebted to Ignatius of Loyola for teaching us how to use all our senses and our imagination in prayer as we pray the life of Jesus.

Apophatic prayer is the reverse of kataphatic prayer. It is receptive, not active; it requires surrender and release, not seeking images and insights. We prepare ourselves for engaging this silence by relaxing our body, focusing our attention, and being present to the Sacred; but we do not take ourselves into this depth of silence. The pathway requires surrender; we must learn to wait; we must listen; we must relinquish control and the direction we travel.

The history of this approach to prayer reaches back to Philo of Alexandria and Pseudo-Dionysius in the early centuries of Christian faith. John of the Cross also wrote extensively about this way of prayer. In more recent times, Thomas Merton, a Trappist monk at Gethsemani Monastery in Bardstown, Kentucky, advocated this rich, but dark path of prayer.

WAYS INTO THE SILENCE

But for those searching for silence, those who are bombarded with the noise of the street and the cries from within, the question is always how: how does one enter into the silence? Here are four ways to explore:

1. Silence the place. Select a quiet place for your retreat. Be aware, however, that most every place generates a low-grade noise. Notice the things in your chosen place that emit sounds, even soft ones: the ceiling fan, the computer, a branch tapping the window or a TV in the next room. Find a place apart from trucks and trains and car horns.

If your place of silence is at home, request those living with you to assist you in finding a period of silence. I find members of the family are usually sensitive to this personal need. If you are in a retreat center or monastery, the host or guest master will gladly request other visitors to be especially sensitive about their noise.

CHRIST IN THE DESERT
May 2007

towering red rocks
cradle a twisting green vale
of quiet and peace

the ridges gazing down
appear unmoved
by the past, present

and future of life
teeming below

yet the vigil of
even the loftiest stone giants
is wonderfully tied
through ribs, buttresses, shoots and
tumble-down slides
finally to bottomlands
where living water runs

river flows, spawning
animal migrations, diseases and fires
sweep and retreat
like armies on a field
before unmoved kings of war

creatures cry out
to the constant heavens and
unchanged pillars of the earth
for mercy and grace
until a rock tumbles down
shed like a tear
echoing to eternity

—Steve Brinn

2. Silence the body. All of us carry within our bodies a degree of pain, tension, and stress—noise. The time spent in relaxing the body and releasing the pent-up tension is never wasted. The following techniques will encourage you to relax your muscles and open yourself to the silence.

- Seat yourself comfortably with feet flat on the floor. Take ten deep breaths. Mentally follow the breath as it comes into your body through your nose or mouth, and visualize it filling your lungs with life and energy. Consciously breathe in, breathe out.

As you are breathing deeply and slowly, begin to identify those places in your body that are tense and tight. Imagine the living breath touching these places and drawing the tension and pain out of them.

- While seated, mentally speak to each part of your body and silence it, request each part to relax and be still. Begin with your toes and visualize all the tension flowing out of your toes, then your feet and ankles. After quieting your feet, silence the tension in your legs from the ankle to the knee. Take your time; feel the tension flowing out of your legs. Do the same for your thighs. Pause for a minute or two and recognize the calm that has come into your legs and feet.

- Again, focus in succession on your buttocks and your groin and stomach. Keep your breathing deep and regular as you tell each of these body parts to become still and quiet. Take your time. There is no rush to get finished with this task. Appreciate the life and health that is coming into your body.

- Mentally visualize each vertebra in your back, moving from your waist up to the top of your neck. Slowly quiet each of these vertebrae. When you have emptied the backbone of tension, picture the tension flowing out of your chest. Keep noticing your breathing. Keep allowing the breath to bring life and empty you of conflict and tension. Pause after you have mentally touched all the parts of your upper body. Let the healing sink in.

- Notice your head, neck, shoulders. Tension collects in these places. Begin with your forehead—relax . . . relax. Focus on your eye sockets and allow all tension to liquefy and begin to flow from your eyes. Give attention to the sides of your head, the top of your head, your neck. Keep breathing life into these members of your body. Now think of the tension and pain in your head becoming liquid. Let it drain from your head into your neck and shoulders. Imagine this liquefied tension flowing down your arms and trickling out through your fingertips.

- Now think of your body as floating in silence. The silence surrounds you; the silence engulfs you; the silence buoys you up; the silence penetrates you. You are in the silence and the silence is in you. This is a pregnant silence; this is a healing silence.
- If you continue this method of relaxation, it will become a habit that takes little effort. After you have gone through this exercise several times, you will begin to make innovations of your own. With practice, this simple discipline will train your body to get quiet when you sit to pray or to seek the silence.

3. Silence the mind. Everyone who has sought to engage the silence has dealt with wandering thoughts. You should expect to have wandering thoughts and unbidden images come into your mind. The mind seems always to be active whether awake or asleep. In our waking hours we experience a constant flow of images that come spontaneously or in response to external stimuli. This flow is natural and normal. So what can we do to silence the mind, to slow down its reactions, and to gain control of our thoughts?

- You will find that quieting the body has a powerful impact on settling the mind. When you have drained the body of tension and stress and have relaxed all your muscles, the invasion of alien thoughts and feelings dimishes. Silencing the body also silences the mind.
- Let distracting thoughts fly by without being captured by them. Note their presence, like a host of blackbirds flying over your head, and return to your silence. When you become still, images will continue to arise in your consciousness. Notice these images and then let go of them. Do not give them your fixed attention!
- Select a word that you can repeat when you find your mind wandering. Choose a short, simple and easily repeated word: *God*, *life*, *hope*, and *love* are examples. This is not a word to think about or to meditate on; use it like a bell you ring to draw your mind back into the silence. In the silence you will be aware of your awareness, and you will begin to be aware of God.

- Try to develop a sense of humor about your wayward, busy mind. Learn to laugh at yourself when you cannot stay with your silence and permit it to do its work within you.
- Trust that God is at work even when you struggle in your search for quiet. Notice what is happening in your life rather than focusing on your feelings. For example, notice an impulse that suggests you not react to an upsetting event, or an awareness of being part of God's story. Sometimes a still small voice says, "Don't say that" or "Don't participate in this."

4. Silence the spirit. There is a silence deeper and more charged than the silence of the body or the silence of the mind—the silence of the spirit. I am pointing to the human spirit, not the Holy Spirit. On the journey into silence, the human spirit is that deepest part of the human psyche; it is that aspect of our being that senses the Presence of the Holy, the Presence of God.

On this journey it does not fall within our power to direct and control the spirit. Movement and direction in the human spirit occur by divine initiative, not as the result of our efforts. This is the apophatic way, the way of darkness and passivity. When we have silenced the body and silenced the mind, silence seems to take on a life of its own. The silence becomes our director; it becomes the magnet that draws us into the depths; it contains and reveals to us the sacred center of our own being.

Sometimes this process to me is somewhat like watching water in a saucepan when the burner has been turned on. As the water heats, it begins to form small bubbles on the side of the pan; minute by minute they multiply. Then one of these bubbles rises to the surface of the water; soon it is followed by another and another. In a matter of seconds the bubbles become numerous. They come with greater numbers and with greater force. They grow from bubbles to tiny eruptions, and then the bubbles are lost in the rolling, boiling water. The water does not boil itself; it is simply responding to the heat of the fire. The water and the heat have become one; they are united and the appearance of the water has been transformed.

Words, emotions, and images are forbidden on this journey. Our spirit cannot capture the Divine Spirit; nor can it compel, enhance, or understand it. In this deepest kind of silence, the holy engulfs the human; it penetrates to the core of our being. The experience is not something other than our self because the self has fused with the divine; it has experienced union with God albeit for just a moment. Neither our self or God is the other; they have become one. This moment is summed up by Angelus Silesius:

> See what no eye can see,
> go where no foot can go,
> choose that which is no choice—
> then you may hear
> what makes no sound—
> God's voice.[2]

AN INVITATION

I was waiting for the technician to call me for a CAT scan when a large man entered the room and sat down. He had come for an MRI—magnetic resonance imaging.

He said to the woman beside him, "I can't do that, I just can't do that! I can't get into that tube and lie there for an hour. I've got claustrophobia, man, I just can't do it today."

Eventually, he asked me whether I had ever had an MRI. I told him that I had had two or three.

"Were you afraid?" he asked.

"No."

"How did you do it?" he inquired.

"I simply lay down, closed my eyes, and prayed."

Then he replied, "I can't be quiet for an hour. I'm going home; maybe another day or maybe I can go up to the hospital and get them to knock me out, but I can't be silent and still for an hour."

You may feel like my friend in the waiting room. You think you can't be quiet for an hour or half hour or even a quarter hour. You can.

And, you can learn to love the silence both within and without. But knowing about silence is not enough. You must engage it, open yourself to it again and again, and explore its many dimensions.

Realizing the need for silence and understanding something about the ways into silence mean nothing until you become silent. I invite you to explore the silence, to let the Spirit of God guide you into the depths of your own spirit and into a profound awareness of the presence of God. In the final analysis, others cannot teach you how to come into the divine silence. Only God can do that. Others can only invite you into the silence. I hope you will consider this invitation seriously. Do not be afraid.

CHAPTER SEVEN

RETURNING FROM TIME AWAY:
15 Watchwords

....

Consciously take your stillness into all areas of your life.

Having returned from numerous retreats, both personal and those I have led, I have accumulated some wisdom about the time following retreat. These insights have come through my own experience, my reading, and from other retreatants. Since these words of counsel will mean the most when they speak to your immediate experience, reread them from time to time and keep them handy.

1. PREPARE FOR REENTRY

During a retreat, especially a day or longer in length, you will likely come to a profound level of quiet. This inner stillness will affect both mind and body. Extended quiet drains the tension from your body so that your feet, arms, and legs become very relaxed. This state of stillness deepens through your practice of mindfulness. Intentionally noting the objects within the reach of consciousness, walking slowly, and paying attention to your body helps you to remain settled.

The practices you engage in during the retreat will also still your mind. Of course, the relaxation of the body quiets the mind. But

Centering Prayer also focuses and frees your mind. When you become centered, your mind is freed from the effort to think or imagine or feel. Your conscious mind enters into the "darkness" of unknowing and rests in the presence of God. This depth of inner silence of the mind and spirit will need to be protected; it should be honored as the meeting place with God. Centering Prayer was developed and is taught by Father Thomas Keating and the Contemplative Outreach organization. The practice involves two twenty-minute periods of silence each day focused on awareness on God. Father Keating encourages all practitioners to return from wandering thoughts to a singular awareness of God. This way of prayer is fully set forth in his book *Open Mind, Open Heart.*

When your retreat has come to an end, therefore, be aware that you are returning to a noisy world, a world of horn blowing and door slamming, of TV and radio, of cell phones and incessant conversation. It's the world you left a few days ago. Reenter it cautiously.

Though there are many sources of noise you cannot control, you can affect some. For example, you can open the door to your car more slowly and lay your luggage gently in the trunk; you can keep the radio off for the reentry period. You can become so aware of the pool of stillness within your heart that you can draw on it as needed.

When you return home, consciously take your stillness into all areas of your life. Trying to impose your silence upon others is not a good idea; let them catch your slower pace, your gentler style, and the gracious way you respond to them in life situations. Return again and again to your center, where you touch the still ground of your being.

2. MINIMIZE SPIRITUAL EXPECTATIONS

Expectations not only prepare you for a retreat, but your imagination can also serve well in the transition back into daily life. However, expectations may also hinder. You may wonder why strong, positive expectations hinder, even undermine, reentry. By *expectation* I mean an image of how your life will be better, happier, or spiritually transformed. Why would images like these not be useful in life beyond retreat?

There are three reasons to modify or control these expectations. First, these images feed your hunger and create an eagerness for spiritual consolations and pleasure. The purpose of a retreat does not center in pleasure, good feelings, or enhanced self-esteem, but in being more open to God's Spirit. Second, these expectations create a sense of disappointment and breed doubt when they are not met. The effort to create your own future places the emphasis on human effort instead of God's. Third, and most important, these images distract you from what is truly occurring in your life. Frequently, when you expect life to become fuller, richer, and more fulfilled, you overlook the reality of what God is actually doing. It is far better to be relatively free of images of how life ought to be in order to live life as it actually is.

When I asked a friend of mine to think with me about the issue of reentry, she had a different point of view on spiritual expectations. "Isn't it helpful to have goals?" she asked. "If after a retreat, I am considering adding or nurturing a spiritual discipline in my life, isn't it important for me to envision my life including that discipline? I believe there is power in positive expectations; there is power in having hope, even if the expectation is never met. Instead of minimizing expectations, perhaps an alternative is to encourage people to hold their expectations lightly. It is such a tricky maneuver to balance the positive energy that expectations bring while at the same time you relinquish them to God."

Yes, it is important to have positive images of yourself and of your practices. They nurture faith and hope, but even if the desires don't materialize, be assured that God is still at work in your life.

As we begin the spiritual journey in earnest, we need to learn early on that whatever occurs in our life is a bearer of God's will. Whether we are confronted with temptation or face doubts or experience dryness, God is in these testy times with us. If we have strong expectations that our post-retreat days will be full of joy and delight, we likely will miss the presence of God that comes in dryness.

When we give up creating our future by our own expectations, we can see more clearly what God is doing in the events of our lives. Expect one thing: God will be present and active in "just what is!"

3. ATTEND YOUR LIFE

When your mind is unencumbered with expectations, your consciousness can notice and respond to the insights and intentions that come unbidden. These occurrences arise spontaneously and exert a powerful influence. Such impulses tend to be "given" to you at times you don't anticipate and carry a self-authenticating conviction. So pay special attention to strong impressions that come to you immediately after your time away. The most transforming moment for you may not be during the retreat but afterward! This possibility makes it critical for you to notice spontaneous ideas the first week or so after the retreat.

This suggestion may seem to contradict what I said about expectations by creating another expectation. Here's what I wish you to recognize: you may not have an "aha!" moment immediately after your retreat; you may not have a special insight. If this revelatory moment does not come, your retreat was not a failure.

Because over the years I have had the experience of God's coming in a special way after the retreat, and because others have reported similar experiences, I urge you to pay attention to your thoughts, what people say to you, and the ordinary events of your life with special care immediately following your time away.

4. LET THE RETREAT CONTINUE

Some people tend to verbalize everything that happened during a retreat. While there may be positive benefits from telling the retreat story, there are also problems with being too vocal. If, for example, you had a profitable time away, narrating all the insights and experiences can make you vulnerable to pride. Perhaps you become the envy of others who kept your children, covered your responsibilities, or in other ways made it possible for you to take time away.

However you relate your new insights to others, you offer only one perspective. No matter how thoroughly you try to identify all the small occurrences on the retreat, much more happened than you are aware of or can put into words.

But more significant than what you may miss by recounting the retreat experience is the potential for cutting off the process of inner transformation. When you conceptualize and articulate the various aspects of your time away, the process of change and transformation often comes to an end.

One of the desert fathers, Diadochus of Photiki, advised keeping some religious experiences to yourself so that talking about them does not cause them to dissipate. In a colorful metaphor, he explained that if the door of a steam bath is left open, the heat rapidly escapes. Similarly, a soul, by saying a lot via the door of speech, may scatter the remembrance of God to the winds. Silence is the mother of the wisest thoughts.[1]

While there may be some dissipation when we talk about our experiences, there are also benefits. Describing what God has done in our lives tends to fix it more permanently. When we share, others also benefit from our experience. And, we should not forget that Jesus encouraged us to confess him publicly.

5. GUARD YOUR REPORT

How you eventually tell others about your experience requires a heightened sensitivity. You might call it the etiquette of sharing the story. For example, a spouse who has not made a retreat may be anxious about what will happen when you spend these four or five days in prayer and reflection. Waiting without a word of what is happening opens the door to all kinds of questions: *What if God calls him/her to a special mission? How will we relate after this experience?* Naturally, the first questions a partner or significant other will ask after the retreat are, "What did you do? How was it?" You may not wish to speak about the event in detail, but you must provide enough information to allay anxiety in someone who loves you. Generally, if you ask for a little time to absorb the meaning of this pilgrimage, your loved one will be obliging.

Often when people have made a good retreat, the tendency is to tell too much. Give those closest to you a break and feed them only a bite at the time. Live your change!

On the other side of this situation you might face disinterest. For example, someone asked me, "What about the alternative, when no one asks you about your retreat, even those closest to you? I have been on retreats several times after which my husband has never asked me anything. While I certainly didn't want to share all of what happened, I felt disappointed not to have an opening to share some of my experience. I suspect there are others who return to their families without much, if any, spiritual acknowledgement from loved ones about their time away."

If you have a similar experience, don't conclude that those close to you are uninterested. You might open a conversation by asking, "May I tell you something that occurred on my retreat that is quite important to me?" Silence upon your return may signify respect for your privacy. A simple rule applies to this situation: ask the persons in your life for what you need or desire.

6. Getting Back into Your Routine

To segue into your normal routine does not require much effort. Everyday habits tend to rise up and grab you all too readily. Getting home, like getting away, must be faced and dealt with. Take care that your daily tasks and your old habits do not squeeze the inspiration out of you. Notice how you ease back into your familiar world. Guard against unconsciously slipping into the land of "forgetfulness."

Do not be surprised when you catch yourself falling back into old attitudes and practices. Self-condemnation will be of no value. Simply acknowledge what is and get on with your life. You are different but not perfect. You are changed in ways that you have not even noticed. Be as gracious to yourself as you are to others.

God is love (1 John 4:8). Read aloud 1 Corinthians 13:4-7 and substitute *God* for the word *love*. Remember you are in God's school of love, and the teacher will provide all the lessons to help you learn the way of incarnate love.

7. RECALL YOUR DISCOVERIES

God's frequent word to Israel was simple and clear: "Remember!" You often find this exhortation in the Psalms. The reason for this reminder is simple: we humans are prone to forget! Just as the people of Israel forgot who brought them out of Egypt, just as they forgot who led them in the wilderness, and just as they forgot the provisions God offered them, we too forget God's liberation, God's guidance, and God's provision for us.

Recollect what came to you during your life reflection. During your quiet time, what did God show you about yourself, your life? What new insight did you receive into the ways of God? What sense of call did you receive? Bring these matters to mind as a source of inspiration and guidance.

You will be aided in the act of recalling by reviewing what you wrote in your journal. Not only will you recapture insights that came to you while on retreat, but also you will see things that went unnoticed at the time of your writing. You will realize more fully how God is at work in your life. In the act of recalling you will find new energy and a deeper sense of God's closeness.

Remember!

8. REVIEW YOUR INTENTION

Toward the end of your retreat you were encouraged to write a rule of life—a list of commitments to be practiced daily, weekly, monthly, and annually. Turn to that entry in your journal and ask yourself these questions:

a. How have I fared in my daily practices? Do I need to revise my original commitment?

b. What did I commit myself to do weekly? What do these commitments mean in my life?

c. During my first month after my retreat, did I find time for a few hours of solitude?

d. What plans would contribute toward fulfilling my annual commitment?

When you find yourself falling short of your intentions, be kind to yourself. Beating up on yourself will not drive you to a better performance; rather, it will tend to discourage you even more. Either adjust your goal to what you can do, or reach for a little stronger discipline. Whatever efforts you make will be rewarded. Keep reminding yourself, *I am who I am! I am who I am! And, I'm grateful for what God is doing within me.*

9. Listen for God

Life is listening for God! A retreat offers a special time for listening, but it is not the beginning or the end of listening. On your retreat, distractions were minimized. A more intense hunger for God grasped your heart. A desire to find intimacy with God gripped your life more firmly. These attitudes of the heart enable you to hear God's word. But what has been your experience of hearing God speak in the ordinary daily routine of life? Does God speak only on special occasions? Has the regimen of the daily routine silenced the voice that desires to speak in you?

Take time to look back, to listen over the time since your break, short or long, and seek to realize what God has been saying to you. You might find it helpful to:

- Think about your memories.
- Recall the texts of scripture that hold meaning for you.
- Review relationships and unexpected encounters you have had.
- Reflect on moments or days of emptiness and the word they communicated.
- Consider this moment as itself a word being uttered to you.
- Never despair when you cannot understand the word God is speaking. Remember that God's first language is silence.

10. Practice Love

How do you know whether your retreat for a few hours—or a few days— has any meaning for your life? By the increase of your love!

We are often misguided in both our searching and our self-evaluation. While we seek experiences of dreams and visions, of ecstasy and revelations, God desires love. So simple, yet so profound: life with God is about love and loving.

Hidden away in a brief letter of John we find this admonition: "Beloved, let us love one another, because love is from God; everyone who loves is born of God and knows God. Whoever does not love does not know God, for God is love" (1 John 4:7-8).

Time away has no meaning at all unless it increases the love of God in your life. The retreat is like a bellows that fans the flame of divine love in your heart so that the warmth of love may spread to those you touch. Look for the spark of love that stirs your heart to care, to reach out, and to touch the life of another. Whether the person before you is a spouse or child or friend or stranger or a needy person on the street, don't miss the chance to love. Missing out on love is missing out on God!

11. Go Forward

From an encounter with God, go forward! One persistent temptation of the spiritual life is seeking to return to a previous experience of God. Often a time away provides an experience of closeness to God. You realize this intimacy at the moment, but upon returning to your ordered (or disordered) life, the memory of peace or stillness or the depth of intimacy becomes greater than the original event itself in your mind. Hard on the heels of these resurrected memories comes the compulsion to recapture that peaceful or joyous moment.

The effort to recapture a previous experience presents the serious soul with two difficulties: first, it is impossible to return; and second, the effort blinds the soul to what God offers in the present moment. Consider the impossibility of returning to a previous state. The lapse of time allows numerous changes in the human psyche. Whatever the

Divine encounter meant in the past, it would not mean the same thing today. Everything changes. There is no place to go back to. Seeking to go back causes you to lose the reality of God in the present. Surrounded by God in the present, leave the God who is to search for the God who was. The point of meeting, the place of fulfillment, is in the present moment, so it is far superior to remain in the moment and find God in "just what is."

12. SEEK HELP

Sometimes when people go inward, they encounter issues that have been hidden from daily awareness. Memories of conflict, pain, and failure, may not have been constructively processed or healed but, instead, pushed into deeper levels of consciousness. They lie there like anchors attached on the seabed. But when the mind gets still, when the pressure of turbulence has given way to quiet, these old memories often float to the mind's surface. When this occurs, people may choose to deal with them or press them back down again.

Likely, if you refuse to face the pain and confusion of past events, they will continue to haunt you. The wisdom way leads you into these rejected parts of the self with an invitation to face them, own them, and embrace them as a part of your life. Once they are accepted and integrated or healed, they lose their power. Refusing to face these unconscious fears permits them to become monsters of the deep.

Perhaps this has not been your experience; it may even sound alien to your experience, but if you are struggling with guilt or shame, or fears about your future, face the truth and resolve it. If you cannot find a way to extricate yourself from these weights on the soul, seek out a trusted friend with whom you can talk. Hearing yourself acknowledge these old issues will help, and a trusted friend can bring wisdom to your struggle. Also you might find benefit from consultation with a pastoral counselor or a spiritual director. Both have training and skill to aid the process of healing.

13. JOIN COMPANIONS ON THE WAY

Consider finding someone to be a companion on your spiritual journey. At first this suggestion may sound strange to your ears. *What is the purpose of having a spiritual friend to talk with?* you wonder. *What would I speak about with such a person?* Most of us who have never had a friendship like this have asked similar questions.

A spiritual companion is someone you look up to, someone whom you trust. Generally, you judge this person to be farther down the road than you. This companionship would provide an opportunity to state your experience of God to someone; it would let you hear your articulation; it would assist you to clarify the next steps on your journey with God. Normally, a spiritual guide will ask questions more than offer answers. Finding a mature friend who is willing to talk with you will take time, so don't be discouraged when he or she doesn't immediately appear. Part of the selection is the adventure of prayerfully considering different persons and talking with them about your desire for guidance.

Having a friend like this will help you avoid pitfalls; it will spare you times of loneliness; it will give you a sense of accountability. The search for a spiritual friend is worth beginning immediately.

14. KEEP A JOURNAL

You began a journal on your retreat. Continue to keep it. Write in it three or four times each week. The exercises recommended for your retreat illustrate the value of a journal. This personal record becomes a companion, much like a mute, warm personal friend. In it you acknowledge your questions. You note insights from scripture. Sometimes you write your prayers and longings. Often God's guidance will come to you while you are writing about these heartfelt personal matters.

Your journal also becomes the record of your spiritual journey. Having an ongoing account of your transactions with God gives specific content to the narrative of your spiritual journey. It gives you an opportunity to review issues you've faced and resolved, which not only helps you retain your insights but also provides encouragement in hard times. So often we forget these bits of encouragement if they are not written.

To gain these benefits, aim to write in your journal daily, and if you manage to do it three of four times each week, be satisfied. Each month as you review your journal, note issues you have faced and insights you have gained. At the end of each year, review your writing and see what remains yet unresolved for you. Praying about God's agenda for you at the beginning of the year will help you structure this new chunk of time that has been given to you.

15. KEEP YOUR PERSONAL DISCIPLINE

If you were to attend a banquet and enjoy a delicious meal, would you fast until you attended another banquet? Just so, a retreat cannot suffice for daily sustenance. Three basic foods will aid your spiritual health.

Reading the Bible daily. It is not how much you read but how well you listen to what you read. Just one verse that is read thoughtfully and reflectively can nurture the spirit more than breezing through a whole chapter or more.

Praying daily. Ancient Jews prayed three times daily, as do today's Orthodox Jews. Muslims pray five times daily. And members of the Order of Saint Benedict pray seven times daily. If you can set aside only ten minutes, use them to become still, become centered, and express your gratitude for God's presence and blessing. Use every meal as a moment to remember God and to be grateful. Commit your life to God as the first and last act of the day.

Creating pockets of silence. Noise fills your day. Find ways to limit it: turn off the radio sometimes when you are traveling; fast from television for an hour or an evening; escape from family and friends for a few minutes; be with others without talking (listen); occasionally stop by a church and sit quietly in a pew remembering God and the worship that occurs in that place; and, occasionally get up early or stay up late simply to embrace a bit of silence.

Epilogue

I hope this book has led you to discover the meaning of retreats and the value they hold for our lives today. Perhaps you have prepared and planned a retreat because you have been convinced that you need time away in order to infuse regular time with meaning and focus.

If you have not yet made a retreat, begin with a few hours and then work your way into longer periods. Your life will be different. Time away transforms ordinary time into extraordinary time.

The fifteen watchwords—suggestions or reminders—will support you in translating your time away into daily life back home, aid you in keeping the spark of love alive, and help you strengthen your spiritual discipline. An old saying highly applicable to the issues we are confronting holds a lot of wisdom: "Plan your work and work your plan!" It is my prayer that you will discern the wisdom in what we have offered in this volume and adapt it to your life.

Appendix A

LESSON PLANS FOR A CLASS
ON PERSONAL RETREATS

The text of *Time Away* can be of great value in introducing personal retreats to a congregation. A spiritually mature leader can gather a small or large group and use the following lesson plans to

- acquaint persons with the purpose of a retreat,
- instruct them in preparation and planning, and
- suggest ways to reenter the world of everyday living.

The first four sessions discuss the basics of retreat; the fifth session invites the group to practice two of the offices that would be experienced on a monastic retreat—lauds and compline.

The method of instruction is interactive. The instructor serves as a facilitator rather than a lecturer. Each session includes a review of the content of the chapters, an opportunity for personal reflection, exercises that engage each person, and practical outcomes for the whole group. To teach these sessions effectively, be sure each participant has a book; find a quiet place for the meetings; have newsprint or a whiteboard on hand and an iPod or other player with music downloaded for praying the Divine Offices.

SESSION I

Prior to the session, ask participants to read chapters 1 and 2 in the book. Open the session with prayer. State the purpose of the session: *to define the meaning and different aspects of a retreat.* Invite participants to write responses to the questions below and record the group's responses on newsprint or whiteboard.

1. What scripture passages do you remember that refer to the desert or the wilderness? What does the desert mean or symbolize?
2. What did the desert teach Brother Carlo?
3. What do the three retreats described by the author suggest to you? What issue was he dealing with in each of those times away? How have you dealt with such questions?
4. Recall the retreat stories shared by different people throughout the book. Which one speaks most to you and your need for a retreat?

Conclude the session with three or four minutes of silence. Ask participants to bow their heads and pray silently.

Session II

Prior to the session, ask participants to read chapters 3 and 4 in the book. Open the session with prayer. State the purpose of the session: *to give guidance in the preparation for a personal retreat.* Ask participants to respond to the three questions below and write the responses on a whiteboard or on newsprint.

1. What kinds of preparation does the text suggest you make for a retreat? What do you think could be added?
2. Why is preparation necessary for a more meaningful retreat?
3. What part of the preparation would you find difficult? Why would this component be difficult for you?

Review the plans for the various retreats in the text. Then form sub-groups of about four persons each and direct each person to design an overnight retreat. As a minimum, the plan should include: preparation, place, length of travel time, food, and spiritual resources (Bible, books, etc.). Participants may use the format in the text as a guide, but encourage people to adapt to fit their needs and interests. When people have completed the task, ask them to share their plans with one another in the small groups. This interaction may lead to useful revisions.

Bring people back into the large group. Invite responses to the exercise. Conclude the session with five minutes of silence.

SESSION III

Prior to the session, ask participants to read chapters 5 and 6 in the book. Ask a different person in the group to open the session with prayer. State the purpose of the session: *to underscore the different aspects of a monastic retreat.* Invite the group to respond to the questions below and record the group's responses on newsprint.

1. How do you feel about going to a monastery or convent for prayer?
2. How does a monastic retreat differ from a personal retreat at a conference center, cabin, beach house, or campsite?
3. What surprised you about the Liturgy of the Hours (Divine Office, Breviary) and its use in the life of the monastery?
4. Review the names and descriptions of the eight Daily Offices with the group (see pp. 67–69). What do you notice about the scripture themes embodied in Daily Offices?
5. How does participation in the Liturgy of the Hours contribute to prayer and drawing closer to God?
6. To better understand monastic, review the Liturgy for Lauds and Compline in appendix B.

After this session, if it is at all feasible, take your group to a monastery or convent to experience firsthand what the text has described. Make advance arrangements; request the guest master to show you around and explain how daily worship is conducted and how you can participate. All monasteries are happy to provide the service to non-Catholics and Catholics alike.

In preparation for session 4, ask participants to select a passage from their own reading or one of the quotations featured in the book to share with the group at the next meeting.

Spend five minutes in silence reflecting on the session.

SESSION IV

Prior to the session, ask participants to read chapter 7 in the book. When you gather, spend three minutes in silence. Ask members of the group to offer prayers of thanksgiving. After several have given thanks, ask the group to pray for guidance in making a personal retreat.

State the purpose of the session: *to identify a number of issues that cluster around reentry after a period of retreat.*

If the group is twenty or more, divide into smaller groups of four or five. In the small groups have different people read aloud the fifteen watchwords from chapter 7 and invite comments. When the smaller groups have finished, gather into a large group and underscore the insights you have gained.

After this discussion, invite people to share a reading they find particularly meaningful. They need not read the selection; ask them to identify it and explain what it says to them.

Ask the group to discuss how the material in these two lessons may be useful to a person on retreat. Make a list of these possibilities.

Close the session with five minutes of silence together.

SESSION V

Prior to the session, ask participants to review appendix B in the book and go online to listen to the music. Open the session with prayer. Turn to appendix B and read through the Liturgy for Lauds and Compline.

For this session you will need to go online to http://www.upperroom.org/time_away_music/ You can listen to the audio recording of either Lauds or Compline through your Web browser. Or, if you prefer, you can download the audio files by clicking the Subscribe button. You'll need the software program iTunes in order to subscribe to the podcast of the files. iTunes can be downloaded for free from www.apple.com/itunes/ and is compatible with both Macintosh and Windows Operating Systems. You can also use iTunes to burn the files onto a CD for use in your car or on retreat.

Divide your large group into two smaller groups and have them face each other. Begin the music and sing antiphonally.

Appendix B

THE OFFICES OF LAUDS AND COMPLINE

LAUDS

OPENING SENTENCES *Psalm 51:15, Lamentations 3:22-23*

Music: Paul H. Lang

HYMN *The Lord's Abiding Steadfast Love*

Hymn tune: Tramps and Hawkers
Text: Paul H. Lang

Note on Chanting the Psalms: In the following pages you'll see "psalm tones," or chants, for some texts. If this singing style is unfamiliar, these suggestions will get you started. (1) Sing gently with the aim of blending voices. (2) For a long phrase on a single tone, sing in the cadence of natural speech. You may feel awkward at first, but you will improve quickly.

How to follow the music: Accent marks (′) indicate the syllable where you change to the next pitch in the psalm tone. The asterisk (*) indicates you continue the next line on the same pitch.

PSALMS

PSALM 146   *Praise of God's Faithfulness*

Al - le - lu - i - a,   Al - le - lu - i - a,—   Al - le - lu - i - a,   Al - le - lu - i - a.

Psalm Tone

Alleluia!
Praise the Lord, my soul.*
I will praise the Lord all mý life,
and make music to my God as long as Í live.

Do not place your trust in thé powerful,
mortals in whom there is no sálvation.

When their breath leaves them, they return to thé dirt
In that day all their pláns perish.

Happy are those whose help is the God óf Jacob:
whose hope is in the Lord théir God,

Who made the heavens ánd earth,
the seas and all they cóntain.

It is the Lord who is steadfást, faithful;
who is just to the óppressed.

It is God who feeds bread to thé hungry,
the Lord who sets prisonérs free.

The Lord opens blind eyes;*
the Lord raises up the óppressed;
the Lord loves thé just.

The Lord keeps watch over the strangers;*
the Lord restores the orphans ánd widows,
But the way of the wicked is bent tó ruin.

The Lord reigns fórever.
The God of Zion for all genérations.

Alleluia.

SILENT REFLECTION

PSALM 29 *The Glory of God Seen in the Storm*

Attribute to the Lord, you children óf God,
Attribute to the Lord honor ánd glory;
Attribute to the Lord the honor due hís name.
Bow down before the Lord clothed ín holiness.

The Lord's voice is upon thé waters.
The God of glory thunders,*
the Lord thunders over imménse waters;
the voice of the Lord great wíth power,
the voice of the Lord great wíth splendor.

The voice of God bréaks cedars
The Lord shatters the cedars óf Lebanon.
He makes Lebanon skip about like á calf
And Sirion like a wíld ox.

The voice of the Lord cleaves forth with flames óf fire.
The voice of the Lord makes the wilderness whirl;*
the Lord's voice shakes the wilderness óf Kadesh;
the Lord's voice makes the hinds calve, and strips the forést bare;
And in his temple they all sáy, "Glory!"

The Lord sits above thé flood,
Enthroned as King fórever.
May the Lord strengthen hís people;
may the Lord bless his people wíth peace.

Praise the Father, the Son, and the Holý Spirit
both now and fórever.
The God who is, who was, and who is tó come
at the end of thé ages.

SILENT REFLECTION

SCRIPTURE READING   *Lesson from the Daily Lections*

LORD'S SUPPER (optional; see liturgy on pages 116–119)

CANTICLE   *The Song of Zechariah*
                Cantor sings verses OR *All read verses (page 114).*
                All sing refrain below.

Benedictus Refrain

Through your holy prophets, you promised of old
to save us from our enemies,
from the hands of all who hate us,
to show mercy to our forebears,
and to remember your holy covenant. [Refrain]

This was the oath God swore to our father Abraham:
to set us free from the hands of our enemies,
free to worship you without fear,
holy and righteous before you,
all the days of our life. [Refrain]

And you, child, shall be called the prophet of the Most High,
for you will go before the Lord to prepare the way,
to give God's people the knowledge of salvation
by the forgiveness of their sins. In the tender
compassion of our God the dawn from on high shall
break upon us, to shine on those who
dwell in darkness and the shadow of death,
and to guide our feet into the way of peace. [Refrain]

PRAYER TO CONSECRATE THE DAY

Gracious God, we worship you in awe of your power and in praise of your wisdom. You have made all things well. In joyful thanksgiving we begin the day in worship and turn now to offer you this day of our lives as a living sacrifice. We covenant to glorify you:

- by what we say . . .
- by what we love . . .
- by whom we honor and obey . . .
- by how we do our work . . .

As we covenant to glorify you by our life and labor, we are mindful of those you have called us to serve and love:

- the poor and marginalized . . .
- the captives of every kind . . .
- the oppressed and abused . . .
- the weary and disheartened . . .

Take our lives and make them fruitful that you might be glorified and we might continue to grow in grace. In the name of the Father and of the Son and of the Holy Spirit. Amen.

THE LORD'S PRAYER

(See musical setting on pages 120–21.)

Our Father in heaven, hallowed be your name, your kingdom come, your will be done, on earth as it is in heaven. Give us our daily bread. Forgive us our sins as we forgive those who sin against us. Save us from the time of trial and deliver us from evil. For the kingdom, the power, and the glory are yours now and forever. Amen.

DISMISSAL (Deuteronomy 6:4-9)

Leader: Hear this, people of God! The Lord your God is one, and you shall love the Lord with all your heart and all your soul and with all your strength.

People: We will ponder the faith when we rise up and as we walk through the day and when we lie down again—teaching the faith to our children.

Leader: May the strength of God sustain you and the Spirit of God direct you today and always.

People: Amen.

People exchange signs of peace as they depart.

THE LORD'S SUPPER

THE WORD PROCLAIMED

INVITATION TO THE LORD'S TABLE

THE GREAT PRAYER OF THANKSGIVING

Leader: The Lord be with you.
People: And also with you.

Leader: Lift up your hearts.
People: We lift them up to the Lord.

Leader: Let us give thanks to the Lord our God.
People: It is right to give our thanks and praise.

Leader: It is truly right and a great joy to offer you our praise and thanksgiving, creator of all things, sovereign of all time and of every place. In wisdom you have made all things well. Your breath of life sustains every living thing. You formed us from the dust and fashioned us in your image, giving us the wealth of all creation to till and to keep for you. You made us to love and serve you as we love and serve all of your people everywhere.

  Though we rebelled against you, seeking our own way and refusing to live as your obedient and grateful children, you did not disown us, but continued to claim us as your people and call us to return home. You sent your prophets to warn us of the folly of our ways and to call us back to faithfulness.

  When the time was right, out of your love for all creation, you sent your only Son, our Lord, to live among us full of grace and truth, healing our brokenness and calling us to follow in his way. By his obedient sacrifice we are redeemed.

  Therefore we lift up our voices in praise of you, joining with the heavenly hosts and with brothers and sisters in Christ everywhere to sing of your greatness. With all of the mothers and fathers of faith, the angels, the prophets, the apostles, the martyrs, and all of the faithful of every time and place we sing to the glory of your name:

Sanctus

Text: © 1988 English Language Liturgical Consultation (ELLC). www.englishtexts.org
Music: Paul H. Lang and John Holter

You are holy, O God, and blessed is your Son, our Lord, Jesus Christ. In Jesus, your Word became flesh, living among us and knowing our joys, pains, and temptations. He embodied your love, healing the sick, binding up the broken, feeding the hungry, bringing sight to the blind, and announcing the arrival of your kingdom among us. He gathered disciples, taught them the good news of your love by word and deed, and sent them out into the world as ambassadors of your reconciliation.

Dying on the cross, he gave himself in compassion for the world. Rising from death he gave victory to us over all things, even the grave. Death has lost its sting because nothing can separate us from the love of God in Christ Jesus our Lord. Seated now with you in glory, our Lord guides us in the way of faithfulness. We praise you that Christ is glorified, and will come again to fulfill the promise of your kingdom.

The Words of Institution may be said here.

Remembering your grace made tangible in Jesus Christ, we take from your creation the gifts of bread and wine and feast joyfully as we reflect on his dying and rising, and await the day of his return. In gratitude we offer to you our very selves as a living and holy sacrifice, and commit ourselves to follow in Christ's way of obedient service.

Great is the mystery of faith:

Christ has died,
Christ is risen,
Christ will come again.

Gracious God, pour out upon us and upon this bread and this cup your Holy Spirit, that the bread broken and the cup blessed may be the body and blood of Christ. Grant us communion with you and with Christ, that we may be one with all of those who share this feast throughout all time and in every place. As we receive Christ's body, send us out into the world as the body of Christ to love and serve you faithfully, always.

Prayers of Intercession may be spoken here.

Fulfill in us, O God, your will, and strengthen us as we work to fulfill your eternal purpose in all the world. Work through us and guide us in faithfulness as we await the coming of Christ in ultimate triumph, that we may join in the feast of all your saints in the joy of your eternal kingdom.

Through Christ, with Christ, in Christ, in the unity of the Holy Spirit, all glory and honor are yours, almighty Father, now and forever.
Amen.

THE LORD'S PRAYER

(See musical setting on pages 120–21.)

THE BREAKING OF THE BREAD
Hear now the Words of Institution: *(Lifting and breaking the bread)*
The Lord Jesus, on the night when he was handed over, took bread, and after giving thanks to you, he broke it, and gave it to his disciples, saying: "Take, eat. This is my body, given for you. Do this in remembrance of me."

In the same way he took the cup, saying: *(Pouring the wine visibly and lifting the cup)* "This cup is the new covenant sealed in my blood, shed for you for the forgiveness of sins. Drink all of you of it."

Whenever you eat this bread and you drink this cup you proclaim again the Lord's death until he comes.

COMMUNION OF THE PEOPLE
(Service continues on page 122.)

The Lord's Prayer

Text: © English Language Liturgical Consultation (ELLC). www.englishtexts.org
Music: Paul H. Lang

The Prayer of Sealing

Bless the Lord, O my soul;
> **and all that is within me, bless God's holy name!**

Bless the Lord, O my soul,
> **and forget not all God's benefits.**

> Gracious God, as the many grains were mixed and ground together to be the bread, and as the grapes from many vines were joined to make the wine, so we have come from our many places to join together in communion with one another and with you. May the bread we have received build us up as the Body of Christ. May the wine we have poured sustain us as we pour ourselves out in ministry for you. Send us now, in the power of your Spirit, to proclaim your love by word and deed to all the world. **Amen.**

COMPLINE

Opening Sentences *Psalm 124:8*

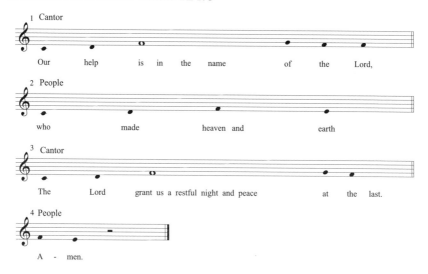

1 Cantor

Our help is in the name of the Lord,

2 People

who made heaven and earth

3 Cantor

The Lord grant us a restful night and peace at the last.

4 People

A - men.

At Close of Day

Text: Paul H. Lang
Music: Arrangement of Ar Hyd Y Nos by Paul H. Lang and Sarah B. Lang

PSALM 4 *Night Prayer*

Show favor to me when I cry out, O God óf justice;
in my distress you made space for me; be gracious and héar my
    prayer!

How long, O people, will you insult mý honor;
will you pursue emptiness and líft up lies?

The Lord distinguishes those who aré kind.
The Lord hears me whenevér I call.
When enraged do not sin,*
search your inner heart while on your bed and keép silence.
Offer a just sacrifice and trust ín the Lord.
Many ask, "Who will show us sóme good?"
May the light of your face shine on ús, O Lord.

You have filled my heart with múch joy;
more than those with plenty of corn ánd new wine.

I will lie down and sleep ín peace,
for in you alone, Lord, I ám in safety.

Praise the Father, the Son, and the Holý Spirit
both now ánd forever.

The God who is, who was, and is tó come
at the end óf the ages.

SILENT REFLECTION

PSALM 91   *Under the Wing of God's Protection*

Those who dwell in the shelter of the Móst High
and lodge in the shade of thé Almighty

say to the Lord: "My refuge ánd fortress;"
my God in whóm I trust!"

It is God who will rescue you from the Fowlér's trap,
from the pestilence which threatens tó destroy you;

His pinions will cover you ín safety,
and in the shelter of his wings you wíll find refuge.

You will not fear the dread of thé night
nor the arrow that fliés by day,
nor the plague that stalks in thé darkness
nor the pestilence that lays wáste at noon.

Though a thousand fall at your side,*
a multitude fall at your ríght hand,
you it will nót come near.

You need only open yoúr eyes
to see how the wicked áre repaid,

Because the Lord is yoúr refuge,
the Most High ís your dwelling.

Upon you no evil wíll come,
no peril come intó your home.

For he will command hís angels,
to guard you in áll your ways.

Their hands shall bear yóu up,
that you not dash your fóot on stone.

Upon lions and snakes you wíll tread
and trample the young lion ánd the dragon.

Those who love me, I wíll save.
I will raise up those who knów my name.

When they call I wíll answer them.
I will save them in the time of trial and bríng them glory.

With length of days I wíll satisfy you;
I will let you see mý salvation.

Praise the Father, the Son, and the Holý Spirit
both now ánd forever.

The God who is, who was, and is tó come
at the end óf the ages.

Silent Reflection

Versicle and Response   *Psalm 17:8*

Guard us, O Lord, as the ap-ple of your eye.

Al-le-lu-ia. Hide us in the shad-ow of your wing. A-men.

CANTICLE OF MARY

Mary's Song

Text: Paul H. Lang, based on Luke 1:46-55
Music: Arrangement of Resignation CDM by Paul H. Lang and Sarah B. Lang

song continues next page

Mary's Song
(continued)

tell,_____	great__ things,	the__ Lord,	up -
pow'r._____	And__ from	be - low	our
cure._____	Through - out	the__ earth	in

on	me__ pressed,	my__ heart	and	soul	are	well.
God	does__ lift	the__ low -	ly	up	that	hour.
ev -	'ry__ land	the__ love	of	God	is	sure!

COLLECT

Peaceful God, you say to us, "Peace I leave with you; my peace I give to you. . . . Do not let your hearts be troubled and do not let them be afraid." Instill in us this hour such peacefulness that with ease we can commit to your care everything which would make us troubled or afraid. As we rest, may we come into that deeper communion with you which heals our wounds and encourages our faith—that we might arise from our rest eager to serve you in faithfulness. We ask this in the name of our risen Lord, the Prince of Peace. Amen.

HYMN *Our Day Complete*

FINAL BLESSING

Go now in peace to love and serve the Lord, who though he was equal to God did not consider his position as something to be exploited — but rather emptied himself in sacrificial service to all. May his peace enfold you. May his strength sustain you. May his Spirit befriend you. May his calling define you. May the all-powerful Lord grant us a restful night and a peaceful death. Amen.

Our Day Complete

Tenderly

1. As the sun flees to the west,— so to bed we now re - tire. Close our eyes and take our rest,— pray the Spir - it to in - spire. From our ac - tive, live - ly la - bor, and all bus - y - ness re - treat. Come to rest with in God's fa - vor, be at peace our day com - plete.

2. Though the world in tu - mult ra - ges, and this life is full of cares, though the strife en - dures for a - ges, join in song; let's sing our prayers. God keeps vig - il while we sleep;— we need nev - er fear the night. In God's love our rest is deep;— God's love makes the dark as light.

3. All God's chil - dren God em - bra - ces, bids us come and en - ter rest. Come to know God's man - y grac - es, in God's arms we know we're blessed. These we ask of you, O Lord:— full nights and peace - ful deaths. Held with - in your love out - poured, let us come to ho - ly rest.

4. As the sun flees to the west,— so to bed we now re - tire. Close our eyes and take our rest,— pray the Spir - it to in - spire. From our ac - tive, live - ly la - bor, and all bus - y - ness re - treat. Come to rest with in God's fa - vor, be at peace, our day com - plete.

(Alternate third stanza)
All God's children, God embraces, bids us come and enter rest.
Come to know God's many graces, in God's arms we know we're blessed.
Like the virgin mother, Mary, held the Christ child to her breast,
God, who's faithful, does not tarry, bids us sup and take our rest.

Text: Paul H. Lang
Music: Arrangement of Suo Gan by Paul H. Lang and Sarah B. Lang

Appendix C

A RETREAT LEADER'S RESOURCE

R etreat leaders have their own styles and ways of guiding a group
on retreat. Though this is not a text on retreat leadership, much
of the material in this book can be helpful to a resourceful leader. It has
been tested in personal retreats, classes, the certificate program at
Columbia Theological Seminary, and in larger group retreats. This
appendix offers suggestions and hints of ways that various aspects of
this book can be used with larger numbers retreating together. Here are
a few thoughts to get you started.

- Ask retreatants to read the first four chapters of this book before
  you gather. In this way, the retreat can begin with them before
  they leave home, and the time away will unfold more fruitfully.
- Offer the definitions and descriptions of retreats to prompt
  retreatants in defining what their retreat is about. Direct people
  to browse the descriptions of retreat experiences highlighted in
  chapters 1 and 2. Invite them to read these as stimulants to their
  thinking and then to write their hopes for their own retreat.
- Here are three ways to use Dr. Sangster's guide to prayer (see pp.
  42–43): (1) Work with the whole group if it is twenty or less.
  Read or describe each movement in prayer, beginning with
  Adoration. After a few moments of silence, invite three or four
  people to say prayers of Adoration. Continue this pattern with
  Thanksgiving, Dedication, Guidance, and Petition. Reserve
  Intercession for last and ask each person to pray aloud for the
  person on his or her right. As the leader, begin the prayer for the
  person on your right, and let it continue until each person has
  been prayed for. (Be sure to give people permission to pray for
  the person in silence and say amen when he or she has finished.)

(2) With groups of four to five people, ask each person to pray each type of prayer beginning with Adoration. Never mind if people confuse Adoration with Thanksgiving. The final prayer of Intercession will be the same as recommended for large groups: pray for the person on your right.

(3) Combine this form of prayer with the directed journaling experience described in point 5 for the overnight retreat on page 48. After you guide people in journaling about what is taking place in their lives, invite them to pray silently about their life using each of the forms cited above: to adore God, thank God, confess to God, seek guidance from God, make requests for themselves, and make intercession for others. Each of these forms of prayer is to be connected with specific parts of their lives. This has been a significant experience for many.

- Choose from the various journaling exercises in the five-day retreat and use them with your group. Each exercise enables persons to deal with different issues in their lives.

The first exercise, "The Turning Points of Your Life," directs people in setting forth and observing the flow of their lives. Some will have done this exercise previously, but there is value after doing it a hundred times; life constantly changes, which means the markers o change. This experience will be most effective early in the retreat.

The second exercise, "The Chapters of Your Life," assists the retreatant in gathering together larger pieces of their life and examining the nature of what took place during particular periods. This gathering encourages them to recognize God's hand in their lives.

The third exercise, "Signs of Grace/ Moments of Pain," guides participants in discovering both negative and positive experiences that have shaped them. As people make this focused life review, they often discover that there was grace in pain and pain in times of grace. This exercise aims to help people let go of residual pain.

The fourth exercise, "Listening to a Chapter of Your Life," promotes a deeper examination into a particular period of life. This time of writing enables persons to connect their inner and outer worlds, to note how the events in the world affected their inner experience.

The fifth exercise, "Guidance from Friends," helps people identify an issue for which they need guidance. The exercise directs attention to those persons who have been mentors and guides, and it draws on these mentors' wisdom to clarify a current issue.

As a retreat leader, you may read the instruction written in the text to facilitate this experience for a group. Be sure to read slowly, giving time for people to think, to receive inspiration, and to express themselves in writing. Don't attempt to use these exercises until you have personally done them!

- The quotations from Carlo Caretto and other writers illustrate many basic points about the spiritual journey. You might wish to use quotations to prompt meditation or discussion or for particular invitations you wish to offer the group. Use your own imagination to find ways of engaging retreatants with this wisdom.
- Every retreat needs closure and wisdom about transitioning back into the ordinary world. In chapter 7, "Returning from Time Away," you will find suggestions regarding this transition. Don't try to discuss all of these suggestions with the group but select those that seem most pertinent and present them to the group for conversation.
- Writing a Rule of Life is a starting point for good habits that enrich the spiritual life. See the outline on the last day of the five-day retreat for guidelines in writing this rule. Briefly, the rule states one's intentions for each day, each week, each month and each year. It answers the question *What spiritual practices will you incorporate in my life?*
- Review all the material in each of the retreat formats offered in chapter 4, "Creating a Plan for Your Retreat," paying special attention to the flow of the suggestions. You need not copy these retreat guides, but the sequencing offers insights into what comes first, middle, and last.

A Retreat Leader's Tasks

- Prepare yourself both mentally and spiritually for leadership of any retreat. Prepare mentally through serious study, and spiritually through prayer.

- Begin with information and exercises that meet people where they are in spiritual development. Give people exercises they can do with confidence. For example, if you wish people to experience silence, teach them how to become still and focused.

- Encourage participants to get to the retreat mentally and physically. Do all you can in arranging the retreat to minimize interference from the outside during the time away.

- Take care in how you structure the activities: for instance, intersperse talks with silence, small-group interaction, quiet walks, and times of prayer. Create a pathway for the group that feels connected and conveys a sense of progress with each new exercise or talk.

- Be careful not to overload the group with too much information. The retreat is about God and the individual. Support each person in remaining focused on the spiritual basis for the retreat.

- Aim to talk personally with everyone at the retreat. Make yourself available when retreatants approach you to talk.

- In your presentations talk *with* people, not *at* them.

- Include some members of your group in planning the retreat; it is always good to have them assume responsibilities.

- Many who go on retreats struggle when it comes to praying aloud. Be careful not to embarrass them. Teach people in small groups to hear their own voice in prayer. To give them experience, invite people to pray mental prayers, then one-word prayers, then sentence prayers, and then conversational prayer. A one-word prayer would be "help" or "forgive." Sentence prayers are: "Thank you for life"; "Guide me in my vocation." Conversational prayer begins with a short prayer by a member of the group, and others add their sentences on the same or a new subject.

- Teach people to listen for God. The chapter on silence (chapter 6) provides material and exercises in listening to the Spirit.
- As the leader, stay present to the process. Don't try to control it but work with what is going on. This means be prepared to change your plan. The people are more important than the plan.
- Ask participants to share in the leadership by reading scripture, leading small groups, relating portions of their personal narratives, and guiding the group in prayer.
- Know when to sit down and when to stand up; know when to speak and when to keep quiet.
- Never let silence control you. Be patient when nothing seems to be happening in a group or in a discussion. Don't let feeling uncomfortable push you into speaking or activity.
- As a facilitator, it is your role to prepare the way for people to experience God. Keep focused on this single, simple task.

A BIBLIOGRAPHY
of Wisdom

When you plan a daily time for quiet reflection, thoughts from spiritual writers can give you focus and inspiration. Such readings can be used both during and after a retreat for renewal and guidance. The Guides to Prayer series published by Upper Room Books offers an excellent collection. The sidebar quotations in chapters 3 and 4 come from these volumes (see details on page 142).

In each of these volumes, daily readings are arranged around a theme and scripture. Compiled by Rueben Job and Norm Shawchuck, this series includes *A Guide to Prayer for Ministers & Other Servants* (1983), *A Guide to Prayer for All God's People* (1990), and *A Guide to Prayer for All Who Seek God* (2003). You will be introduced to writers ancient and modern who comment on the spiritual life, and you will begin to learn which ones especially speak to you in meaningful ways. I recommend these guides to prayer as excellent resources for growing in your spiritual life. Here are more resources:

Anonymous. *The Cloud of Unknowing: And the Book of Privy Counseling.* Edited by William Johnston. Garden City, NY: Image Books, Doubleday, 1973.

Bourgeault, Cynthia. *Centering Prayer and Inner Awakening.* Cambridge, MA: Cowley Publications, 2004.

————. *The Wisdom Way of Knowing: Reclaiming an Ancient Tradition to Awaken the Heart.* San Francisco: Jossey-Bass, 2003.

Carretto, Carlo. *The Desert in the City.* Translated by Barbara Wall. New York: Crossroad, 1982.

————. *I Sought and I Found: My Experience of God and the Church.* Translated by Robert Barr. Maryknoll, NY: Orbis Books, 1983.

————. *Letters from the Desert:* Translated by Rose Mary Hancock. Maryknoll, New York: Orbis Books, 1972.

Caussade, Jean-Pierre de. *Abandonment to Divine Providence.* Translated by John Beevers. New York: Image Books, 1975.

Finley, James. *The Awakening Call.* Notre Dame, IN: Ave Maria Press, 1984.

————. *The Contemplative Heart.* Notre Dame, IN: Sorin Books/Ave Maria Press, 2000.

Ignatius of Loyola. *The Spiritual Exercises of St. Ignatius.* Translated by Anthony Mottola. Garden City, NY: Image Books, 1964.

Jager, Willigis. *The Way to Contemplation: Encountering God Today.* Translated by Matthew J. O'Connell. New York: Paulist Press, 1987.

Johnson, Ben Campbell. *The God Who Speaks: Learning the Language of God.* Grand Rapids, MI: William B. Eerdmans Publishing, 2004.

Keating, Thomas. *Open Mind, Open Heart, The Contemplative Dimension of the Gospel.* New York: Continuum, 1994.

Kelly, Thomas R. *A Testament of Devotion.* New York: Harper & Brothers, 1941.

Lawrence, Brother, and Frank C. Laubach. *Practicing His Presence.* Edited by Gene Edwards. Jacksonville, FL: Seedsowers, 1973.

Merton, Thomas. *Contemplative Prayer.* Garden City, NY: Image Books, 1996.

————. *The Inner Experience: Notes on Contemplation.* Edited by William H. Shannon. San Francisco: HarperSanFrancisco, 2003.

————. *New Seeds of Contemplation.* Norfolk, CT: New Directions, 1961.

Pennington, M. Basil. *Centering Prayer: Renewing an Ancient Christian Prayer Form.* Garden City, NY: Image Books, 1980.

Progoff, Ira. The Symbolic and the Real: *A New Psychological Approach to the Fuller Experience of Personal Existence.* New York: McGraw-Hill, 1963.

St. John of the Cross. *Ascent of Mount Carmel.* Garden City, NY: Image Books, 1973.

The Psalms: The Grail Translation, Inclusive Language Version. London: HarperCollins Publishers, 2009.

Teresa of Avila: The Interior Castle. Translated by Kieran Kavanaugh and Otilio Rodriguez. New York: Paulist Press, 1979.

Notes & Sources

CHAPTER 1
1. Carlo Carretto, *Letters from the Desert*, trans. Rose Mary Hancock, anniversary edition (Maryknoll, NY: Orbis Books, 2002), xvi–xvii, 11, 33.

2. Henri J. M. Nouwen, *The Way of the Heart: Desert Spirituality and Contemporary Ministry* (New York: Seabury Press, 1981), 26–27.

3. James O. Hannay, *The Wisdom of the Desert* (London: Methuen, 1904), 206, as quoted in Nouwen, *The Way of the Heart*, 43.

CHAPTER 2
1. Anthony de Mello, *Awareness: A deMello Spirituality Conference in His Own Words*, ed. J. Francis Stroud (New York: Image Books, 1992), 31.

CHAPTER 4
1. W. E. Sangster, *Teach Me to Pray* (Nashville: Upper Room Books, 1959, 1999), 29–30.

CHAPTER 5
1. Augustine, *Confessions*, Book IX, chapter 6.

CHAPTER 6
1. Romano Guardini, *Meditations before Mass*, trans. Elinor Castendyk Briefs (Westminster, MD: Newman Press, 1959).

2. Angelus Silesius, *Messenger of the Heart: The Book of Angelus Silesius*, trans. Frederick Franck (Bloomington, IN: World Wisdom, 2005), 113.

CHAPTER 7
1. Diadochus of Photiki, in *The Philokalia*, vol. 1 (London & Boston: Faber & Faber, 1979), 276, as quoted in Nouwen, *The Way of the Heart*, 52–53.

SOURCES FOR QUOTATIONS

The sidebar quotations in chapters 3 and 4 come from the Guides to Prayer series (Upper Room Books). Noted here are the original source and the specific Guide to Prayer in which each quotation appears.

Page 37: from *A Guide to Prayer for All Who Seek God* by Norman Shawchuck and Rueben P. Job (Nashville: Upper Room Books, 2003), 69.

Page 41: from *The Reasons of the Heart: A Journey into Solitude and Back Again into the Human Cycle* by John S. Dunne (New York: Macmillan, 1978), quoted in *A Guide to Prayer for Ministers and Other Servants.*

Page 42: from *Freedom of Simplicity: Finding Harmony in a Complex World* by Richard J. Foster (New York: HarperCollins, 1981), quoted in *A Guide to Prayer for All God's People.*

Page 49: from *The God Who Comes* by Carlo Carretto (London: Dartman, Longman and Todd, 1981), quoted in *A Guide to Prayer for Ministers and Other Servants.*

Page 50: from *Open Mind, Open Heart* by Thomas Keating (New York: Continuum, 2006), quoted in *A Guide to Prayer for All God's People.*

Page 52: from *The Double Search* by Rufus Jones (Richmond, IN: Friends United Press), quoted in *A Guide to Prayer for Ministers and Other Servants.*

Page 55: from *The Imitation of Christ* by Thomas à Kempis, quoted in *A Guide to Prayer for All God's People.*

Page 58: from *Merton's Palace of Nowhere* by James Finley (Notre Dame, IN: Ave Maria Press, 1978), quoted in *A Guide to Prayer for All God's People.*

Page 61: from *Yearning to Know God's Will* by Danny E. Morris (Grand Rapids, MI: Zondervan, 1991), quoted in *A Guide to Prayer for All Who Seek God.*

Page 62: from *Listening Hearts: Discerning Call in Community* by Suzanne G. Farnham et al. (Harrisburg, PA: Morehouse), quoted in *A Guide to Prayer for All Who Seek God.*

About the Authors

BEN CAMPBELL JOHNSON is professor emeritus of Christian spirituality at Columbia Theological Seminary in Decatur, Georgia. He taught evangelism and Christian spirituality for twenty years, retiring in 2000. Ben has been on the cutting edge of renewal movements in the church: small groups in the 1960s; lay renewal and lay ministry in the 1970s; evangelism and church growth in the 1980s; spirituality and personal growth in the 1990s; and, in the early years of the twenty-first century, contemplation and interfaith work. He has authored more than forty books on these subjects. His journal and resources related to interfaith conversations can be found at www.bencampbelljohnson.com.

Ben is married to Nan Baird Johnson, a supportive companion in all of these renewal endeavors. Together Ben and Nan have reared five children who now have families of their own and have blessed them with seven grandchildren.

PAUL H. LANG is pastor of Peace Presbyterian Church in Winterville, North Carolina. A graduate of Furman University (BA, Music), Paul continued his studies at Columbia Theological Seminary where he earned a Master of Divinity degree in 1993 and a Doctor of Ministry degree in 2003. He received the Lyman and Myki Mobley Prize in Biblical Scholarship for his paper on the use of musical settings of the Psalms in Christian worship.

In 2008 Paul used a Lilly Foundation grant to travel throughout Europe and the United States visiting monasteries where the Liturgy of the Hours is being used. He leads retreats and workshops in a variety of settings. Paul and his wife, Sarah, live in Greenville, North Carolina, with sons Daniel and Benjamin. To hear some of the music Paul has created visit www.paulhlang.com.

Related Resources from
Upper Room Books

The three Guides to Prayer edited by Rueben P. Job and Norman Shawchuck referred to in this book are

A GUIDE TO PRAYER FOR MINISTERS AND OTHER SERVANTS
ISBN 978-0-8358-0559-9

A GUIDE TO PRAYER FOR ALL WHO SEEK GOD
ISBN 978-0-8358-1001-2

A GUIDE TO PRAYER FOR ALL GOD'S PEOPLE
ISBN 978-0-8358-0710-X

CREATING A LIFE WITH GOD:
THE CALL OF ANCIENT PRAYER PRACTICES
Daniel Wolpert
ISBN 978-0-8358-9855-5

FORTY DAYS TO A CLOSER WALK WITH GOD:
THE PRACTICE OF CENTERING PRAYER
J. David Muyskens
ISBN 978-0-8358-9904-8

OPENINGS: A DAYBOOK OF SAINTS, PSALMS, AND PRAYER
Larry James Peacock
ISBN 0-8358-9850-4

Visit us at www.upperroom.org/bookstore

Books are also available at your local bookstore
or by calling 1.800.972.0433